T0345174

# DeepFakes

DeepFakes is a synthetic media that leverages powerful Artificial Intelligence (AI) and machine learning (ML) techniques to generate fake visual and audio content that are extremely realistic, thus making it very hard for a human to distinguish it from the original ones. Apart from a technological introduction to the DeepFakes concept, the book details algorithms to detect DeepFakes, techniques for identifying manipulated content and identifying face swap, generative adversarial neural networks, media forensic techniques, deep learning architectures, forensic analysis of DeepFakes, and so forth.

- Provides a technical introduction to DeepFakes, its benefits, and the potential harms
- Presents practical approaches of creation and detection of DeepFakes using Deep Learning (DL) techniques
- Draws attention toward various challenging issues and societal impact of DeepFakes with their existing solutions
- Includes research analysis in the domain of DL fakes for assisting the creation and detection of DeepFakes applications
- Discusses future research directions with the emergence of DeepFakes technology

This book is aimed at graduate students, researchers, and professionals in data science, AI, computer vision, and machine learning.

# DeepFakes
## Creation, Detection, and Impact

Edited by
## Loveleen Gaur

**CRC Press**
Taylor & Francis Group
Boca Raton  London  New York

CRC Press is an imprint of the
Taylor & Francis Group, an **informa** business

First edition published 2023
by CRC Press
6000 Broken Sound Parkway NW, Suite 300, Boca Raton, FL 33487-2742

and by CRC Press
4 Park Square, Milton Park, Abingdon, Oxon, OX14 4RN

*CRC Press is an imprint of Taylor & Francis Group, LLC*

© 2023 selection and editorial matter, Loveleen Gaur; individual chapters, the contributors

*Library of Congress Cataloging-in-Publication Data*
A catalog number has been requested for this title.

ISBN: 978-1-032-13920-3 (hbk)
ISBN: 978-1-032-13923-4 (pbk)
ISBN: 978-1-003-23149-3 (ebk)

DOI: 10.1201/9781003231493

Typeset in Times
by Newgen Publishing UK

*This book is dedicated to my family, friends, students, and all those who have inspired me directly and indirectly.*

# Contents

# Preface

It gives me immense pleasure to put forth the book title *"DeepFake: Creation, Detection, and Impact."* One of the most frightening applications of deep learning algorithms creating buzz nowadays is "DeepFakes." It is a recently developed deep learning-powered application. DeepFakes could be an image, audio, or video content that appear extremely realistic to humans, specifically when used to generate and alter/swap images of faces. The algorithms can create fake photos and videos that humans cannot distinguish from the original ones. It is a combination of "deep learning and fake." Fake videos are developed with the help of Artificial Intelligence (AI) and incredibly Generative Adversarial Networks (GANs) software, to depict people doing or saying things that they have never done. These videos may seem quite realistic.

The pervasive use of image-sharing social media platforms provides a large amount of data combined with deep learning techniques, especially GANs, to produce DeepFakes that appear authentic. It can potentially create misleading and explicit content, with predominantly influential personalities such as celebrities, politicians, and even religious leaders being targeted. The concept is evolving quickly and is becoming dangerous, not just for the victims' reputation but also for their security. In this challenging scenario, algorithms are needed to unmask the DeepFakes, detect them, or, at least, to mitigate the potential harm and abuse that can be done by employing these multimedia contents.

This book is very appropriate in these exceptional times. The book summarizes the trends and impact of receiving altered versions of oneself and others by using DeepFakes technology. The book also sums up how exposure to DeepFakes undermines trust in media; how technological immersion interacts with DeepFakes; the endurance and resilience of DeepFakes; strategies around debunking or countering DeepFakes; and understanding the use of DeepFakes in self-presentation during social interaction. I firmly believe that this critical reference source is ideal for researchers, academicians, practitioners, companies, and students.

## CHAPTER 1: INTRODUCTION TO DEEPFAKE TECHNOLOGIES

The chapter introduces the concept of DeepFakes tools/technologies for creating and detecting DeepFakes. It builds the foundation for the readers to understand the current usage of DeepFakes in business.

## CHAPTER 2: DEEPFAKES: A SYSTEMATIC REVIEW AND BIBLIOMETRIC ANALYSIS

The chapter focuses on a systematic literature review, identifying the main approaches that are currently available to identify fake media and applying them in different situations. This chapter focuses on the top journals and leading countries having scientific publications on DeepFake.

## CHAPTER 3: DEEP LEARNING TECHNIQUES FOR CREATION OF DEEPFAKES

The chapter focuses on advanced deep learning techniques for the creation of DeepFakes. This chapter aims to create a better understanding to the readers regarding the implementation of deep learning in DeepFakes.

## CHAPTER 4: ANALYZING DEEPFAKES VIDEOS BY FACE WARPING ARTIFACTS

The objective of this chapter is to use face warping artifacts to distinguish DeepFake videos from the real ones effectively and to understand the difference between the two.

## CHAPTER 5: DEVELOPMENT OF IMAGE TRANSLATING MODEL TO COUNTER ADVERSARIAL ATTACKS

The objective of this chapter is to develop a model to countermeasure the misuse of a deep generative model by using adversarial attacks to create subtle alarms that would cause deep generative algorithms to fail in generating the fake image in the first place.

## CHAPTER 6: DETECTION OF DEEPFAKES USING LOCAL FEATURES AND CONVOLUTIONAL NEURAL NETWORK

The chapter analyzes DeepFakes of human faces to detect a forensics trace hidden in the images using local features and a convolutional generative process.

## CHAPTER 7: DEEPFAKES: POSITIVE CASES

This chapter focuses on the point that the importance of DeepFakes is two-pronged; there are various positive use cases of DeepFakes. This chapter aims to identify and analyze the positive side of DeepFakes, i.e., education, speech impediments, and so forth.

## CHAPTER 8: THREATS AND CHALLENGES BY DEEPFAKE TECHNOLOGY

This chapter aims to analyze the impact of various threats and challenges posed by DeepFakes on the society.

## CHAPTER 9: DEEPFAKES, MEDIA, AND SOCIETAL IMPACTS

The chapter brings a comprehensive study on DeepFakes, media, and their impact on geopolitics.

## CHAPTER 10: FAKE NEWS DETECTION USING MACHINE LEARNING

This chapter focuses on advanced DeepFakes techniques for creating fake news.

## CHAPTER 11: FUTURE OF DEEPFAKES AND ECTYPES

This chapter focuses on the future aspects where DeepFakes techniques can be implemented and provide the ectypes where DeepFakes has been implemented.

Digital technologies such as artificial intelligence, machine learning, and deep learning will be vital in how DeepFakes provide business advantages. I thank our esteemed authors for showing confidence in the book and considering it as a platform to showcase and share their original work.

*Editor:*
**Loveleen Gaur,** *Amity International Business School (AIBS)*
*Amity University, Noida, India*

# Acknowledgments

Nothing is more important and urgent than giving thanks. Many individuals have provided their valuable suggestions and criticism, which helped publish the first edition. Dozens of students participated in the various chapter discussions, software applications, problem analyses, and material collection. It is not possible to name everyone who participated in this project, but my thanks goes to all of them. Specific individuals made significant contributions, and hence they deserve a special recognition.

First, I appreciate the efforts of those individuals who provided a formal review of the first edition book.

Adesh Gaur, *Software Development Senior Advisor, NTT Data*

Gurinder Singh, *Group Vice Chancellor, Amity Universities*

Gurmeet Singh, *The University of the South Pacific, Fiji*

Noor Zaman Jhanjhi, *Taylors University, Subang Jaya, Selangor, Malaysia*

Tarun Kumar Singhal, *Christ (Deemed to be University), Delhi NCR Campus, India*

Saurav Mallik, *Harvard University, MA, USA*

I am also grateful to Gagandeep Singh and Aditi Mittal at Taylor and Francis for showing confidence in my work. Without their help, the creation of this book would not have been possible.

Also, I would like to acknowledge with gratitude the support and love of my family—my mother (Amarjeet Kaur), my husband (Adesh Gaur), my daughter (Devanshi Gaur), and my son (Raghav Gaur). They are the pillars and strengths that kept me going—finally, my gratitude to the divine power and HIS blessings.

**Loveleen Gaur**

# Editor Biography

**Loveleen Gaur** is currently working as Professor and Program Director (Artificial Intelligence and Data Analytics) at Amity International Business School, Amity University, India. She has more than 20 years of teaching, research, and administrative experience internationally. She is the founding director of MBA in Artificial Intelligence and Data Analytics in Amity International Business School. She is supervising a number of PhD scholars and postgraduate students, mainly in Artificial Intelligence and Data Analytics for business and management. Under her guidance, the AI/Data Analytics research cluster has published extensively in high-impact-factor journals and has established extensive research collaboration globally with several renowned professionals.

She is a senior IEEE member and Series Editor with CRC and Wiley. She has high-indexed publications in SCI/ABDC/WoS/Scopus and has several Patents/copyrights on her account and has edited/authored more than 20 research books published by world-class publishers. She has excellent experience in supervising and co-supervising postgraduate students internationally. An ample number of PhD and master's students graduated under her supervision. She is an external PhD/master's thesis examiner/evaluator for several universities globally. She has completed internationally funded research grants successfully. She has also served as Keynote speaker for several international conferences, presented several webinars worldwide, and chaired international conference sessions. Gaur has significantly contributed to enhancing scientific understanding by participating in more than 300 scientific conferences, symposia, and seminars, by chairing technical sessions and delivering plenary and invited talks.

# Contributors

**Ratish Agrawal**
Associate Professor,
Department of IT, UIT RGPV
Bhopal, India

**Mohan Bhandari**
Lecturer, NCIT,
Nepal

**Amlan Chakarbarti**
Professor and Director
A.K.Choudhury School of Information
    Technology,
University of Calcutta, Calcutta, India

**Ajantha Devi Vairamani**
Research Head, AP3 Solutions
Chennai, Tamil Nadu, India

**Adesh Gaur**
Senior Software Architect,
NTT Data
Sector 125, Noida, India

**Loveleen Gaur**
Professor and Program Director
Amity International Business
    School,
Sector 125, Amity University,
    Noida, India

**Noor Zaman Jhanjhi**
Associate Professor, Director Center for
    Smart Society 5.0 [CSS5],
Taylor's University, Malaysia

**Gursimar Kaur Arora**
Consultant,
Deloitte USI
Delhi, India

**Srabanti Maji**
Assistant Professor,
DIT University, Dehradun, India

**Saurav Mallik**
Postdoctoral Fellow
Harvard University, MA, USA

**Amit Kumar Mishra**
Associate Professor and Head of the
    School of Computing,
DIT University, Dehradun, India

**Shubha Mishra**
Assistant Professor
Lakshmi Narain College of Technology,
    Bhopal, India

**Jyoti Rana**
Research scholar, Amity College of
    Commerce and Finance,
Sector 125, Amity University,
    Noida, India

**Shreya Rastogi**
Software Engineer,
Xenon Stack
Mohali, Chandigarh, India

**Mansi Ratta**
Business Analyst,
Prospecta Software, Noida, India

**Sonali Raturi**
Scholar, DIT University,
Uttarakhand, India

**Tanvi Razdan**
Business Analyst, Hyundai Motor India
    Limited (HMIL)
Noida, India

**Mamta Sareen**
Head of Department
Delhi University, Delhi, India

**Piyush Kumar Shukla**
Associate Professor, Computer Science
  & Engineering Department, India
University Institute of Technology,
  Rajiv Gandhi Proudyogiki
  Vishwavidyalaya, India

# 1 Introduction to DeepFake Technologies

*Loveleen Gaur, Saurav Mallik, and*
*Noor Zaman Jhanjhi*

## CONTENTS

## 1.1 INTRODUCTION

The current era can be explicitly characterized by digital dominance, where the creation, communication, and dissemination of information are digitally driven. It has raised an alarming and challenging condition of trust and verification of the digital content available for the citizens. AI is a paradigm-shift technology due to its diverse utilitarian functions exhibited in the past years.

The subfield of AI is Deep Learning (DL), which plays a massive role in developing many applications. The catchphrase DF originates from the concealed innovation, i.e., profound realizing—a sort of AI [1]. DF technology is revealing a different age of media production. Like all the other technologies, both constructive and dangerous use cases happen.

As the name suggests, DL be taught from a sizeable amount of data and has many (deep) levels that facilitate learning. Similar to how humans learn from experience, the DL algorithm would repetitively carry out a task, each time adjusting it to enhance the outcome. DL permits machines to unravel complicated problems for disparate, unstructured, and inter-connected datasets. The performance of algorithms depends on in-depth learning. DL has sophisticated capabilities to create or alter images, scripts, and expressions exceedingly practically.

DOI: 10.1201/9781003231493-1

**1**

Intrinsically, DL fuelled the creation of forged texts, artificial tones, counterfeit videos, and faked photographs, all of which may appear astonishingly legitimate and accurate. However, they are not [2].

The contemporary advancements in AI and DL have provided soar to the trend of DFs (formally, a doctored image or video). The trend of the formation of credible doctored online creations is soaring high on social media platforms with lots of falsified pictures and a plethora of videos of celebrities, politicians, and renowned personalities. The risk and the societal implications are substantial and far-damaging, notably with the minimal technical proficiency and devices needed to produce DFs. Such content can be effortlessly generated by anybody and dispersed electronically. Thus, this mandates the thorough investigation of DFs through various lenses, including media, society, digital platforms, viewers, sexual characteristics, law, regulations, and political beliefs. To understand the criticalness of DFs, one must understand the underlying concept. First, this chapter will discuss the idea, origin, history, trends, and impact on the society.

## 1.2  DEMYSTIFYING DEEPFAKES

DeepFake is a collection of "deep learning" and "forgery," which employs DL algorithms to modify images, acoustic, and video to generate a synthetic/phony media. It is a non-autonomous process that applies AI algorithms to subject matter, producing doctored images, video, and audio.

The underlying technology can overlay face images, create facial motions, switch faces, maneuver facial expressions, produce faces, and synthesize the speech of a target individual onto a video of a spokesperson in order to create a video of the target individual acting similarly to the source person. The subsequent impersonation is often practically indistinguishable from the original ones. These tools are applied generally to portray individuals stating or performing something they never do in typical scenarios. DL has vital applications in a type of complex real-world difficulties, varying from big-data analytics computer-vision sensitivity to autonomous control systems. Unfortunately, with the development of DL techniques, risks to the privacy, strength, and safety of Machine Learning (ML)-driven systems have also developed.

## 1.3  ORIGIN AND HISTORY

Computer vision is a complex field largely involved in processing images, providing PCs with the skill to realize knowledge from pictures. The widespread applications include autonomous vehicles, diagnosing diseases in healthcare, and face detection by Facebook for photograph tagging suggestions. DFs technology falls under the umbrella of computer vision.

The foundation of DFs was laid in 1997 when Bregler et al. established the groundbreaking "Video Rewrite Program" [3] that could produce fresh-found facial simulations from an audio output. However, this paper remained the original to lay these three concepts and animate them realistically. It is considered one of the essential works in creating DFs technology groundwork [4].

In 2001, another famous paper by Cootes et al. on the active appearance models (AAM) algorithm was published, which used a comprehensive statistical prototype to fit a shape to an image; a remarkable contribution in face matching and tracking domain [5].

Theis et al. (2016), in their Face2Face, attempt to create an instantaneous animation, swapping the mouth area of its target video with an actor; this video doesn't contain a voice. Similarly, in their paper synthesizing Obama, Suwajanakorn et al. (2017) enhanced the graphical improvements with more animations, textures, and expressions. Although the objectives of both papers were different, these papers improved the handling and translation periods while others are renewing graphic conformity to look photorealistic. These papers are the milestones in developing DFs [6,7]. The term DF was invented in 2017 by a Reddit customer of the identical name. He started posting pornographic images and videos of celebrities using open-source face-swapping technology. Later, Reddit banned the users and updated their content policy. The term has since extended to incorporate "synthetic media applications" and innovative creations such as StyleGAN (images of people that look real but don't exist). The recent trend is moving toward manipulated recorded speech [8,9].

## 1.4 THE GROWING TREND OF DEEPFAKES

With the advancement of AI and computer vision, the trend is moving from celebrities to the public to superimpose prevailing images and videos onto source images or videos using the generative adversarial network (GAN) technique [10].

The trend is growing toward fake videos for political or pornographic purposes. According to the report released by Sensity in 2019, a total of 14,678 DF videos were found online. It is also observed that 96% were used in pornographic matters. The trend is increasing, and the number of DFs is proliferating. Apart from celebrities, popular social media influencers and famous internet personalities are widely targeted. Other than that, originators also aim at people, frequently women, active users. The most apparent threat is posed to women right now with non-consensual pornography. Also, the trend is growing toward false vengeance porn. The danger is not just limited to women; the movement may creep in schools or workplaces, as anybody can put people into absurd, dangerous, or compromising situations. Other worries related to DFs are extortion, identity fraud, big corporations' scams, and danger to democracy [11].

Above and beyond the extensive usage of non-consensual, engineered porn, there is an increase in instances where DFs are employed to imitate somebody attempting to start a bank account. People can fake an ID and their appearances in videos using highly sophisticated algorithms. Although the application of such deception is not prevalent, it does signify an eviller application for DFs. The trend and its widespread impact is believed to continue in times to come with easy accessibility of technology; the regulations and clear policy on the use of AI are critically needed to control the negative aspect [12].

## 1.5  WHY IS IT A MATTER OF CONCERN?

The hue and cry around DF are not unreasonable. It matters due to the following concerns:

- *Seeing is believing*: It is pretty convincing for us to believe in what we see and listen to from our ears. It is unlikely not to believe in the things you have observed yourself. It is now much easier to trick the brain's visual system with misperception by utilizing these booming latest technologies.
- *Availability:* With easy-to-use new apps, it is much easier to create such deceiving content in image, video, or any other form of media. The accessibility is growing with the rise of tools and technologies. For example, the Zao app permits users to place their faces into movie/TV clips.

## 1.6  HOW DOES DEEPFAKES WORK?

The three-step process of any DFs includes the following:

1.  The extraction of the original picture from the original frame.
2.  Using this extracted picture as input to DL algorithms automatically generates the exact match for the original picture.
3.  The rendered picture is then inserted into the original reference image to create a fake photo.

DFs are primarily built using "autoencoder," a deep network architecture [13,14].

Autoencoders are trained to recognize the main features of an input image to recreate it as their output subsequently. In this process, the network performs heavy data compression. The following are the three subparts of autoencoders:

- *Encoder*: It is responsible for extracting critical characteristics from the input image. The encoder compresses the original image from thousands of pixels to hundreds. These measurements are related to facial features such as movement of eyes, head pose, skin tone, emotional expressions, etc.
- *Latent space* represents unique facial features on which the image is trained. It is more focused on critical facial features. It excludes the noise/unimportant part of the image, indicating the picture as a compressed version which ultimately helps in memorizing the essential characteristics.
- *Decoder* decompresses the information in the latent space to reconstruct a lookalike of the original image. The comparison of input and output images provides the performance of the autoencoder. The more the similarity of input and output image, the more the encoder's performance [13,14].

If two separate autoencoders are trained on different people, the integration is difficult to attain. The secret for creating DFs is communicating the encoder across two networks to stay consistent. It means that the image of one person can be used to

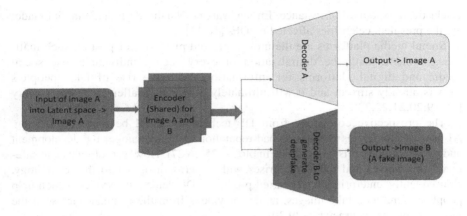

**FIGURE 1.1** Illustration of "How DFs work?"

compute a compressed latent space representation, from where the decoder of another person is used to create the doctored/fake image.

### 1.6.1 ANALYZING THE TECHNOLOGY

Researchers demonstrated that it is easy to define the criteria to identify the DF based on the number of parameters. The specified parameters are as follows:

- Total number of images
- Illumination situations/lighting
- The size and quality of the input
- Position of the input image
- Varying facial forms
- Intersecting objects

## 1.7 INFLUENCE OF DEEPFAKES

DFs are severe AI and ML technology exploitation that can influence and intimidate people and organizations. They are going to inflict turmoil on the society by manipulating the emotions and opinions of people. The unethical use of technology has enduring prospective consequences for the society and its people at large [15].

Political DFs are at the prominent edge of video-based misinformation available online. For example, if left unchallenged, Barack Obama and Donald Trump's popular DFs have profound repercussions for journalism, citizen competence, and the quality of democracy. Circumstantial proof indicates that the possibility of mass production and dissemination of DFs by mischievous people may present a severe challenge to the legitimacy of online political dialogues. It can play a critical role in influencing public belief in the build-up to elections. Another severe corollary of DF is its extensive usage in producing sexually explicit images/videos falsifying the celebrities in spoofs. For instance, Emma Watson, Natalie Portman, and Gal Gadot are the prevalent celebrities affected by DFs [16,17].

Social media platforms are the most preferred platform for posting such malicious content. With the digitalization of every sector, individuals use social media and digital platforms for information. With the rise of DFs, people's trust is already stirred, and it will ultimately pose real challenges to the society [18,19,20,21,22,23,24].

The prospective corollaries from DF technology could be more devastating. AI-based technologies will earn a bad reputation and may hamper the development and growth around this potential technology [25,26,27]. However, officials can safeguard themselves and their enterprises with superior insight into the technology. Consequently, enterprises have started providing DF detection services, which help people differentiate fake images, audio, or videos from the original ones with the most acceptable accuracy [28,29,30].

## 1.8 SUMMARY

Data manipulation is nothing new; it has been the age-old trend when Joseph Stalin used suppression and image editing to influence his character and government in the early-mid 20th century. The remarkable growth of computers has added fuel, and now manipulation is a matter of a few clicks. Also, researchers have demonstrated that individuals have a sharp inclination to have confidence in their own eyes and ears. Thus, when the mass media they consume appears too great to be fake, it's effortless to fall victim to trickery. While "photoshopping" still images has been a stronghold of digital culture, doctored photos and videos of individuals currently progressively discover their way online in the form of DFs.

The next chapter will focus on the related work in DFs. It will also focus on the AI techniques utilized by researchers to create and detect DFs.

## REFERENCES

[1]   Meredith, S. (2019). DFs, Explained, https://mitsloan.mit.edu/ideas-made-to-matter/DFs-explained (Accessed on August 17, 2021).

[2]   Cole, S. (24 January 2018). "We Are Truly Fucked: Everyone Is Making AI-Generated Fake Porn Now." Vice. Archived from the original on 7 September 2019. Retrieved May 4, 2019.

[3]   Bregler, C., Covell, M., and Slaney, M. (1997). "Video Rewrite: Driving Visual Speech with Audio," Proceedings of the 24th Annual Conference on Computer Graphics and Interactive Techniques, 24: 353–360. doi:10.1145/258734.258880

[4]   Karnouskos, S. (Sept. 2020). "AIin Digital Media: The Era of DFs," IEEE Transactions on Technology and Society, 1(3): 138–147. doi:10.1109/TTS.2020.3001312

[5]   Cootes, T.F., Edwards, G.J., and Taylor, C.J. (June 2001). "Active Appearance Models," IEEE Transactions on Pattern Analysis And Machine Intelligence, 23(6): 681–682.

[6]   Westerlund, M. (2019). "The Emergence of DF Technology: A Review," Technology Innovation Management Review, 9(11): 39–54. http://doi.org/10.22215/timreview/1282; https://timreview.ca/article/1282

[7] Thies, J., Zollhöfer, M., Stamminger, M., Theobalt, C., and Nießner, M. (2016). "Face2Face: Realtime Face Capture and Reenactment of RGB Videos," Proc. Computer Vision and Pattern Recognition (CVPR), IEEE, 62(1): 96–104. doi:10.1145/3292039

[8] Thies, J., Zollhöfer, M., Stamminger, M., Theobalt, C., and Nießner, M. (January 2019). "Face2Face: Real-Time Face Capture and Reenactment of RGB Videos," Communications of the ACM, 62(1): 96–104. doi:10.1145/3292039

[9] Suwajanakorn, S., Seitz, S.M., and Kemelmacher-Shlizerman, I., (2017). "Synthesizing Obama: Learning Lip Sync from Audio," University of Washington, https://grail.cs.washington.edu/projects/AudioToObama/siggraph17_obama.pdf

[10] Vaccari, C., and Chadwick, A. (2020). "DFs and Disinformation: Exploring the Impact of Synthetic Political Video on Deception, Uncertainty, and Trust in News," Social Media and Society 6(1): 1–13. https://doi.org/10.1177/2056305120903408

[11] https://blog.gao.gov/2020/10/20/deconstructing-DFs-how-do-they-work-and-what-are-the-risks/ (Accessed on August 17, 2021).

[12] www.nortonlifelock.com/blogs/norton-labs/DFs-terror-era-ai (Accessed on August 17, 2021).

[13] Sharma, D.K., Gaur, L., and Okunbor, D. (2007). "Image Compression and Feature Extraction with Neural Network," Proceedings of the Academy of Information and Management Sciences, 11(1): 33–38.

[14] Singh, G., Kumar, B., Gaur, L., and Tyagi, A. (2019). "Comparison between Multinomial and Bernoulli Naïve Bayes for Text Classification," 2019 International Conference on Automation, Computational and Technology Management (ICACTM), pp. 593–596, doi:10.1109/ICACTM.2019.8776800

[15] https://interculturaltalk.com/2019/11/05/cool-but-scaryDFs-are-here/ (Accessed on August 17, 2021).

[16] https://medium.com/@songda/a-short-history-of-DFs-604ac7be6016 (Accessed on August 17, 2021).

[17] www.discovermagazine.com/technology/DFs-the-dark-origins-of-fake-videos-and-their-potential-to-wreak-havoc (Accessed on August, 17, 2021).

[18] Anshu, K., Gaur, L., and Khazanchi, D. (2017). "Evaluating Satisfaction Level of Grocery E-retailers Using Intuitionistic Fuzzy TOPSIS and ECCSI Model," International Conference on Infocom Technologies and Unmanned Systems (Trends and Future Directions) (ICTUS), pp. 276–284, doi:10.1109/ICTUS.2017.8286019

[19] Gaur, L., and Anshu, K. (2018). "Consumer Preference Analysis for Websites Using e-TailQ and AHP," International Journal of Engineering & Technology, 7(2.11): 14–20.

[20] Gaur, L., Singh, G., Solanki, A., Jhanjhi, N. Z., Bhatia, U., Sharma, S., … and Kim, W. (2021), "Disposition of Youth in Predicting Sustainable Development Goals Using the Neuro-fuzzy and Random Forest Algorithms," Human-Centric Computing and Information Sciences, 11(NA): 1–19.

[21] Gaur L., Agarwal V., and Anshu K. (2020). "Fuzzy DEMATEL Approach to Identify the Factors Influencing Efficiency of Indian Retail," Strategic System Assurance and Business Analytics. Asset Analytics (Performance and Safety Management). Springer, Singapore. https://doi.org/10.1007/978-981-15-3647-2_

[22] Sahu, G., Gaur, L., and Singh, G. (2021). "Applying Niche and Gratification Theory Approach to Examine the Users' Indulgence Towards Over-the-Top Platforms and Conventional TV," Telematics and Informatics, 65. ISSN 0736-5853. doi:10.1016/j.tele.2021.101713

[23] Ramakrishnan, R., Gaur, L., and Singh, G. (2016). "Feasibility and Efficacy of BLE Beacon IoT Devices in Inventory Management at the Shop Floor," International Journal of Electrical and Computer Engineering, 6(5): 2362–2368. doi:10.11591/ijece. v6i5.10807

[24] Afaq, A., Gaur, L., Singh, G., and Dhir, A. (2021). "COVID-19: Transforming Air Passengers' Behaviour and Reshaping Their Expectations Towards the Airline Industry," Tourism Recreation Research. doi:10.1080/02508281.2021.2008211

[25] Rana, J., Gaur, L., Singh, G., Awan, U., and Rasheed, M.I. (2021). "Reinforcing Customer Journey Through Artificial Intelligence: A Review and Research Agenda," International Journal of Emerging Markets, Vol. ahead-of-print (No. ahead-of-print). https://doi.org/10.1108/IJOEM-08-2021-1214

[26] Gaur, L., Afaq, A., Singh, G., and Dwivedi, Y.K. (2021). "Role of Artificial Intelligence and Robotics to Foster the Touchless Travel During a Pandemic: A Review and Research Agenda," International Journal of Contemporary Hospitality Management, 33(11): 4079–4098. https://doi.org/10.1108/IJCHM-11-2020-1246

[27] Sharma, S., Singh, G., Gaur, L., and Sharma, R. (2022). "Does Psychological Distance and Religiosity Influence Fraudulent Customer Behaviour?" International Journal of Consumer Studies. doi:10.1111/ijcs.12773

[28] https://spectrum.ieee.org/what-is-DF (Accessed on August 17, 2021).

[29] www.technologyreview.com/2020/12/24/1015380/best-ai-DFs-of-2020/ (Accessed on August 17, 2021).

[30] https://latinamericanpost.com/34481-what-are-DFs-and-why-are-they-such-a-big-problem (Accessed on August 20, 2021).

# 2 DeepFakes
## *A Systematic Review and Bibliometric Analysis*

*Loveleen Gaur, Jyoti Rana, and Amlan Chakrabarti*

## CONTENTS

## 2.1  INTRODUCTION

DeepFakes (DFs) have been around a long time but have recently gained a lot of interest for good and bad reasons. The following publications have provided a good point of view for what exactly DFs is and a more detailed picture. Kietzmann et al. [1] have talked about what DFs is, the different types of existing DFs, the technology behind them, and what opportunities and problems it poses and can create in the future. To address the issue of DFs, they have also proposed the "REAL framework," a set of principles designed to manage the risks associated with DFs. The framework is intended to expose DFs early, protect individuals, and leverage trust to counter credulity. The authors [2] have explained how DFs have contributed to the rising fake news and disinformation online. After analyzing a sample population based in the UK, they found that people are more likely to feel uncertain than be misled by DFs, but this uncertainty reduces their trust in news sources.

Moving on toward the technical bit of DFs, i.e., how they are created and could be detected. Korshunov and Marcel [3] have given a brief introduction for DFs; they

DOI: 10.1201/9781003231493-2

have then presented a publicly available dataset for DFs and created them via generative adversarial network (GAN). It is found that FaceNet and VGG face recognition systems were vulnerable to DFs and that the audio-visual-based lip consistency method was not that effective in detecting DFs. After conducting and analyzing more procedures, it is concluded that the best approach was, based on the visual quality metrics, producing an error rate of 8.97% for high-quality DFs. Kumar et al.'s [4] study provided a brief overview of recent studies and the datasets used to support the research. They looked at the emergence of DFs and the ways to combat them to facilitate the development of a better and more effective technology and methods to combat the DF issues. Xu et al. [5] provided a unique way by dealing with DFs as a fine-grained classification problem and proposed a multi-attentional DF detection network. Their model consists of three critical concepts that increase the overall efficiency of the model. With intense experiments and training data, they have provided some promising results. Similarly, Huang et al. (2020) [6] have introduced a simple yet powerful framework that reduces the patterns of fake images without impacting the image quality. Their main observation was that "adding noise to a fake image can successfully reduce the artifact patterns in both spatial and frequency domain." They used available data on DFs and created more from various GANs to train and experiment with their framework. Their method aims to improve the fidelity of DFs and expose the problems with existing DFs detection methods. Finally, Hernandez-Ortega et al. [7] has proposed a method for detecting DFs based on heart rate detection. They have used "remote Photoplethysmography" (rPPG) to see the heart rate in the videos. The convolutional attention network (CAN), which is used in their model, gathers spatial and temporal information from video frames, analyzing and combining both sources to detect false films more effectively. This identification method is tested utilizing the most current public databases available in the field: Celeb-DF and DFDC. The results were optimistic, demonstrating the success of physiologically based fake detectors in detecting the most recent DFs.

Ahmed's [8] publication has provided a brief introduction to DFs, the underlying technology. He has focused on highlighting the benefits and threats that DFs pose to businesses, society, and the world. The paper concludes with future directions for DFs.

## 2.2 DATA COLLECTION

The authors used a single keyword, "DeepFakes," for data collection from the Scopus database. The initial search results were 254 for document types such as articles and conferences papers, source types such as journals and conference proceedings, and limited Language to English. The data were retrieved on 26 October 2021 at 2:42 PM as per Indian Standard Time. Figure 2.1 depicts the Scopus search process using the Preferred Reporting Items for Systematic Reviews and Meta-Analyses (PRISMA) flowchart [9].

### 2.2.1 OBJECTIVE OF THE STUDY

The focus of the study is to identify the main domains and the role of DFs in business by answering the following research questions (RQs).

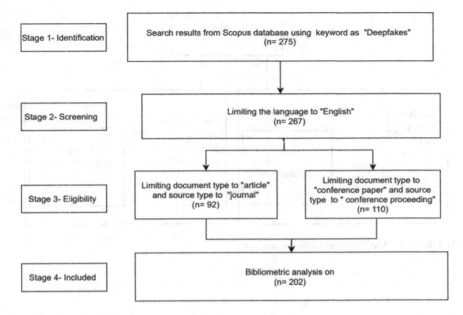

**FIGURE 2.1** PRISMA flowchart search process Scopus.

RQ1: Finding publication trends and critical journals, publishing research articles on the application of DFs in business and domains.

RQ2: How have the DFs studies enhanced their research streams, pointing out the most influential authors and countries?

RQ3: Conduct keyword analysis and co-citation analysis to articles published to integrate DFs in business.

A bibliometric study (as shown in Figure 2.2) provides the researcher with the freedom to systematically plan, organize, and investigate the literature and attain comprehensive knowledge of the field. Bibliometrics is a complete and detailed approach to tracking knowledge anatomy in any research field [10].

## 2.3  FINDINGS AND DISCUSSIONS

### 2.3.1  PUBLICATION TRENDS

Publication trends attempt to find out the publication taking place in the field of DFs over the years. The emergence of DF is a novel concept; hence it has limited studies. The scientific trend of publication of DFs for the past three years is shown in Figure 2.3 [11,12].

The year 2019 bought DF publication in journals and conferences, with 18 publications, followed by 97 in 2020. The upsurge in publications is due to the COVID-19 pandemic, and in the year 2021, until mid-October 2021, had 87 publications [13].

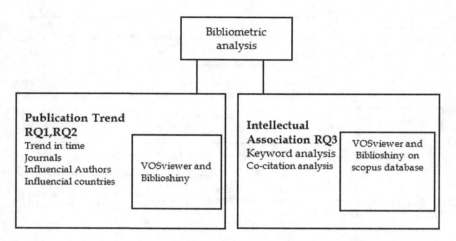

**FIGURE 2.2**    Methods and tools for analysis.

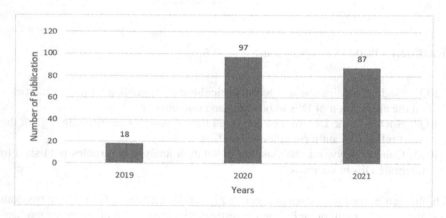

**FIGURE 2.3**    Publication trends.

## 2.3.2    CO-AUTHORSHIP TO AUTHOR

Co-authorship is when two or more persons have made significant contributions to a journal article. The co-author shares responsibility and accountability for the results. Here, the software VOSviewer is used to visualize the Scopus database. The limit of minimum number of documents an author has is set to 3, and the minimum number of citations is also set as 3; out of 582 authors, only 23 authors could meet the threshold. Table 2.1 shows the list of first authors working in the domain of DFs [14].

The same is shown in Figure 2.4, which offers ten connected authors. The figure is created by using the VOSviewer software [15].

They form two significant clusters. Cluster 1, shown in red, has six authors: Rui Wang, Yang Liu, Lei Ma, Felix Juefei-Xu, Xiaofei Xie, and Xi Gou. Cluster 2, shown in green, has four authors: Pu Sun, Hua Qi, Yuezun Li, and Siwei Lyu.

**TABLE 2.1**
**Co-authorship to Authors**

| Authors | Documents | Citation | Link Strength |
|---|---|---|---|
| Honggang Qi | 4 | 68 | 14 |
| Yuezun Li | 4 | 67 | 9 |
| Jiarui Liu | 4 | 3 | 0 |
| Yan Liu | 4 | 11 | 15 |
| Siwei Lyu | 3 | 65 | 9 |
| Pu Sun | 3 | 65 | 9 |
| Ruben Tolosana | 3 | 40 | 3 |
| Julian Fierrez | 3 | 40 | 3 |
| Oliver Giudice | 3 | 23 | 6 |
| Luca Guarnera | 3 | 23 | 6 |
| Sebastiano Battiato | 3 | 23 | 6 |
| Simson S. Woo | 3 | 14 | 0 |
| Qing Guo | 3 | 11 | 15 |
| Felix Juefei-Xu | 3 | 11 | 15 |
| Lei Ma | 3 | 11 | 15 |
| Xiaofei Xie | 3 | 11 | 15 |
| Akash Chintha | 3 | 11 | 6 |
| Matthew Wright | 3 | 11 | 6 |
| Rui Wang | 3 | 9 | 10 |
| Raymond Ptucha | 3 | 11 | 6 |
| Zahid Akhtar | 3 | 8 | 0 |
| Saifuddin Ahmed | 3 | 9 | 0 |
| Jan Kietmann | 3 | 6 | 0 |

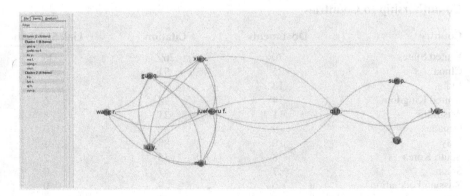

**FIGURE 2.4** Co-authorship to author analysis of ten connected authors.

### 2.3.3 CO-AUTHORSHIP OF ORGANIZATION

Co-authorship of organization analysis is the co-authorship of authors belonging to which organization work in tandem with authors of the other organization. The limit of minimum number of documents of an organization is set as 3, and the minimum number of citations of an organization is also set as 3; out of 326, only 5 could meet the threshold. Table 2.2 shows the list of organizations.

### 2.3.4 CO-AUTHORSHIP OF COUNTRIES

Table 2.3 depicts the list of countries. The limit of minimum documents a country has is set to 3, and the minimum number of citations is also limited to 3; out of 51 countries, only 16 countries could meet the threshold.

**TABLE 2.2**
**Co-authorship to Organizations**

| Organizations | Documents | Citation | Link Strength |
|---|---|---|---|
| University of Chinese Academy of Science, China | 4 | 65 | 0 |
| University of Michigan, United States | 3 | 49 | 0 |
| Alibaba Group, San Mateo, United States | 3 | 11 | 3 |
| Kyushu University, Fukuoka, Japan | 3 | 11 | 3 |
| Nanyang Technological University, Singapore | 3 | 9 | 0 |

**TABLE 2.3**
**Co-authorship to Countries**

| Country | Documents | Citation | Link Strength |
|---|---|---|---|
| United States | 70 | 269 | 26 |
| China | 25 | 91 | 15 |
| India | 18 | 27 | 1 |
| United Kingdom | 14 | 78 | 6 |
| Australia | 11 | 21 | 8 |
| Canada | 9 | 36 | 10 |
| Italy | 10 | 88 | 1 |
| South Korea | 8 | 35 | 2 |
| Spain | 7 | 47 | 0 |
| Russian Federation | 6 | 9 | 0 |
| Singapore | 6 | 20 | 9 |
| Germany | 5 | 155 | 0 |
| Netherlands | 4 | 11 | 3 |
| Japan | 3 | 11 | 9 |
| Ireland | 3 | 3 | 0 |
| Norway | 3 | 5 | 0 |

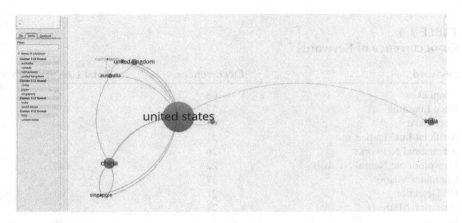

**FIGURE 2.5** Co-authorship to countries analysis of 11 connected countries.

Out of the 16 countries, only 11 countries are connected, as shown in Figure 2.5.

### 2.3.5 Co-occurrence of Keywords

Keyword means a word or concept of significance; here, the authors provide the co-occurrence of keyword analysis based on the minimum number of times a keyword occurred, which is set as 10. Out of 1263 keywords, only 19 keywords could meet the threshold; the same is shown in Table 2.4. As per the VOSviewer, link strength is a positive numerical value of each link. A strong connection means a higher value.

The keywords that occurred at least ten times in the dataset are shown in Table 2.4; the same is depicted by Figure 2.6, forming three significant clusters of keywords.

### 2.3.6 Bibliographic Coupling of Authors

Bibliographic coupling is used in all fields. It helps researchers find the related work of the past studies. When two documents refer to a third typical work in their references, the probability exists that two pieces share the same domain. Here, Table 2.5 has a list of authors found in the references list. The minimum number of documents an author has was limited to 3, and the minimum number of citations an author has is also limited to 3.

Out of 582 authors, only 23 authors could meet the threshold. The same is shown in Figure 2.7; the 23 authors had three significant clusters.

### 2.3.7 List of the Prominent Journals

The most prominent journal list is based on the number of publications. The list is made using the Biblioshiny software. Here, the authors have purposefully only mentioned the name of journals that have more than one article published in the domain of DFs. Table 2.6 shows the list of 16 journals publishing more than one research article in the field of DFs.

**TABLE 2.4**
**Co-occurrence of Keywords**

| Keyword | Occurrences | Total Link Strength |
|---|---|---|
| DeepFakes | 68 | 82 |
| Deep Learning | 57 | 144 |
| Deep Fake | 41 | 80 |
| Artificial Intelligence | 31 | 59 |
| Adversarial Networks | 26 | 79 |
| Convolutional Neural Networks | 22 | 47 |
| Computer Vision | 27 | 48 |
| DF Detection | 21 | 41 |
| Detection Methods | 21 | 52 |
| State of Art | 18 | 49 |
| Face Recognition | 15 | 32 |
| Social Media | 15 | 26 |
| Deep Neural Networks | 16 | 33 |
| GANs | 13 | 39 |
| ML | 12 | 23 |
| Fake News | 11 | 29 |
| Learning Systems | 12 | 36 |
| Convolution | 10 | 31 |
| Disinformation | 10 | 19 |

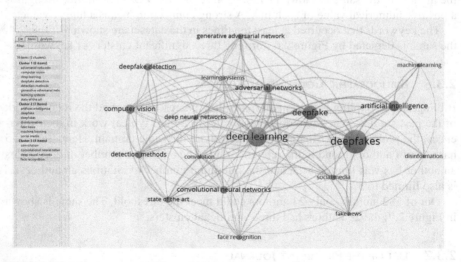

**FIGURE 2.6**   Co-occurrence of keywords.

**TABLE 2.5**
**Bibliographic Coupling of Authors**

| Authors | Documents | Citation | Total Link Strength |
|---|---|---|---|
| **Cluster 1 (10)** | | | |
| Ruben Tolosana | 3 | 40 | 331 |
| Julian Fierrez | 3 | 40 | 331 |
| Sebastiano Battiato | 3 | 23 | 710 |
| Oliver Giudice | 3 | 23 | 710 |
| Luca Guarnera | 3 | 23 | 710 |
| Simson S. Woo | 3 | 14 | 451 |
| Matthew Wright | 3 | 11 | 1104 |
| Raymond Ptucha | 3 | 11 | 1104 |
| Akash Chintha | 3 | 11 | 1104 |
| Jan Kietmann | 3 | 6 | 22 |
| **Cluster 2 (7)** | | | |
| Honggang Qi | 4 | 68 | 1023 |
| Yuezun Li | 4 | 67 | 551 |
| Jiarui Liu | 4 | 3 | 436 |
| Siwei Lyu | 3 | 65 | 482 |
| Pu Sun | 3 | 65 | 482 |
| Saifuddin Ahmed | 3 | 9 | 14 |
| Zahid Akhtar | 3 | 8 | 196 |
| **Cluster 3 (6)** | | | |
| Yang Liu | 4 | 11 | 1620 |
| Felix Juefei-Xu | 3 | 11 | 1471 |
| Qing Guo | 3 | 11 | 1471 |
| Lei Ma | 3 | 11 | 1471 |
| Xiaofei Xie | 3 | 11 | 1471 |
| Rui Wang | 3 | 9 | 1011 |

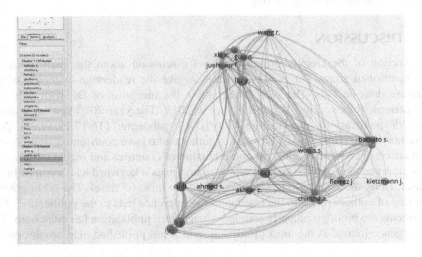

**FIGURE 2.7**   Bibliographic coupling of authors.

**TABLE 2.6**
**List of Journals Publishing More than One Article**

| Journal Name | Articles Published |
|---|---|
| *Convergence* | 9 |
| *Porn Studies* | 7 |
| *IEEE Access* | 4 |
| *Cyber Psychology Behaviour and Social Networking* | 3 |
| IEEE Journal on Selected Topics in Signal Processing | 3 |
| *International Journal of Advance Trends in Computer Science and Engineering* | 2 |
| *International Journal of Press/Politics* | 2 |
| *IT Professional* | 2 |
| *Journal of Visual Communication and Image Representation* | 2 |
| *Journal of Imaging* | 2 |
| *Journal of Visual Communication and Image Representation* | 2 |
| *Media and Communication* | 2 |
| *Moral Philosophy and Politics* | 2 |
| *New Media and Society* | 2 |
| *Philosophy and Technology* | 2 |
| *Russia in Global Affairs* | 2 |

The convergence journal is noted to be the most prominent, which has published nine articles on the domain of DFs.

### 2.3.8 LIST OF PROMINENT CONFERENCES

The list of major conferences is made the same way as the list of journals here. Also, in Table 2.7, only those conferences have published more than one conference paper, and only 15 could make up the list.

## 2.4 DISCUSSION

This section of the chapter provides a brief discussion about the analysis of the aforementioned areas. The publication trends give the readers an overview of the literature done in DFs. The year 2018 bought the inception of DF with only two publications, followed by 18 publications in 2019. The year 2020 saw an upsurge with 98 publications due to the COVID-19 pandemic [16,17,18,19,20]. The co-authorship to author analysis provides authors who have contributed significantly to an article. The same follows for co-authorship of countries and organizations. The co-occurrence of keywords indicates how many times a keyword has occurred in the dataset. Here, the keyword "DF" has appeared the most 65 times. The bibliographic coupling of authors refers to the overlap in the reference lists to the publication. Two documents are bibliographically coupled when a third publication has cited both. The convergence journal is the most prominent, which has published nine articles on the

**TABLE 2.7**
**List of Conferences Publishing More than One Document**

| Conference Name | Documents Published |
| --- | --- |
| IEEE Computer Society Conference on Computer Vision and Pattern Recognition Workshops | 8 |
| MM 2020 – Proceedings of the 28th ACM International Conference on Multimedia | 5 |
| Proceedings – Applied Imagery Pattern Recognition | 5 |
| CEUR Workshop Proceedings | 5 |
| IS and T International Symposium on Electronic Imaging Science and Technology | 4 |
| Proceedings of the IEEE Computer Society Conference on Computer Vision and Pattern Recognition | 3 |
| ACM International Conference Proceedings Series | 2 |
| Conference on Human factors in Computer Systems-Proceedings | 2 |
| ICASSP IEEE International Conference in Acoustics Speech and Signal Processing-Proceedings | 2 |
| Proceedings – 2021 IEEE Winter Conference on Application of Computer Vision WACV 2021 | 2 |
| Proceedings of the International Joint Conference on Neural Networks | 2 |
| Proceedings – 5th International Conference on Computing Methodologies and Communication ICCMC 2021 | 2 |
| Proceedings of the 4th International Conference on IoT in Social Mobile Analytics and Cloud ISMAC 2020 | 2 |
| Proceedings of the European Conference on the Impact of AI and Robotics Éclair 2020 | 2 |
| The Web Conference 2021 – Proceedings of the World Wide Web Conference WWW 2021 | 2 |

domain of DFs, followed by *Porn Studies* and *IEEE Access* [21,22,23]. The influential conferences are IEEE Computer Society Conference on Computer Vision and Pattern Recognition Workshops, MM 2020 – Proceedings of the 28th ACM International Conference on Multimedia, Proceedings – Applied Imagery Pattern Recognition, and CEUR Workshop Proceedings, publishing five documents.

## 2.5 SUMMARY

In the conclusion of the earlier analysis, it can be said that although the inception of DFs has initiated in the year 2019, it has been applied in many fields such as Computer Science, Engineering, Social Science, Arts, Humanities, Decision Science, Psychology, Physics, and Astronomy [24–30]. DF is still an evolving concept, and countries worldwide, whether developed or developing, are using it; hence, researchers can gain knowledge on the application of DFs, keeping in mind the privacy issues. Just like the two sides of a coin, utilizing DFs in business will possess pros and cons. Therefore, the business houses should have a detailed analysis and conduct a pilot study to understand customers' perception and trust in DFs.

The next chapter will discuss the algorithms used for the creation of DFs.

## REFERENCES

[1] Kietzmann, J., Mills, A.J., and Plangger, K. (2021). DFs: Perspectives on the Future "Reality" of Advertising and Branding. International Journal of Advertising, 40(3), 473–485. doi:10.1080/02650487.2020.1834211

[2] Vaccari, C., and Chadwick, A. (2020). DFs and Disinformation: Exploring the Impact of Synthetic Political Video on Deception, Uncertainty, and Trust in News. Social Media and Society, 6 (1). doi:10.1177/2056305120903408

[3] Korshunov, P., and Marcel, S. (2019). Vulnerability Assessment and Detection of DF Videos. 2019 International Conference on Biometrics. doi:10.1109/ICB45273.2019.8987375

[4] Kumar, P., Vatsa, M., and Singh, R. (2020). Detecting Face2Face Facial Reenactment in Videos. Proceedings – 2020 IEEE Winter Conference on Applications of Computer Vision, WACV 2020. doi:10.1109/WACV45572.2020.9093628

[5] Xu, Z., Liu, J., Lu, W., Xu, B., Zhao, X., Li, B., and Huang, J. (2021). Detecting Facial Manipulated Videos Based on Set Convolutional Neural Networks. Journal of Visual Communication Image Representation, 77 doi:10.1016/j.jvcir.2021.103119

[6] Huang, Y., Juefei-Xu, F., Guo, Q., Xie, X. & Ma, L., Miao, W., Liu, Y., and Pu, G. (2020). FakeRetouch: Evading DeepFakes Detection via the Guidance of Deliberate Noise, 70.

[7] Hernandez-Ortega, J., Tolosana, R., Fierrez, J., and Morales, A. (2021). DFsON-Phys: DFs Detection Based on Heart Rate Estimation. CEUR Workshop Proceedings.

[8] Ahmed, S. (2021). Fooled by the Fakes: Cognitive Differences in Perceived Claim Accuracy and Sharing the Intention of Non-political DFs. Personality and Individual Differences, 182(111074). doi:10.1016/j.paid.2021.111074

[9] Liberati, A., Altman, D.G., Tetzlaff, J., Mulrow, C., Gøtzsche, P.C., Ioannidis, J.P.A., Clarke, M., Devereaux, P.J., Kleijnen, J., and Moher, D. (2009). The Prisma Statement for Reporting Systematic Reviews and Meta-analyses of Studies That Evaluate Healthcare Interventions: Explanation and Elaboration. BMJ, 339.

[10] Rana, J., Gaur, L., Singh, G., Awan, U., and Rasheed, M.I. (2021). Reinforcing Customer Journey Through Artificial Intelligence: A Review and Research Agenda. International Journal of Emerging Markets, Vol. ahead-of-print (No. ahead-of-print). https://doi.org/10.1108/IJOEM-08-2021-1214

[11] Pavis, M. (2021). Rebalancing Our Regulatory Response to DFs with Performers' Rights. Convergence, 27(4), 974–998. doi:10.1177/13548565211033418

[12] Lees, D., Bashford-Rogers, T., and Keppel-Palmer, M. (2021). The Digital Resurrection of Margaret Thatcher: Creative, Technological and Legal Dilemmas in the Use of DFs in Screen Drama. Convergence, 27(4), 954–973. doi:10.1177/13548565211030452

[13] Bonomi, M., Pasquini, C., and Boato, G. (2021). Dynamic Texture Analysis for Detecting Fake Faces in Video Sequences. Journal of Visual Communication and Image Representation, 79 . doi:10.1016/j.jvcir.2021.103239

[14] Jung, H., Green, A., Morales, J., Silva, M., Martinez, B., Cattaneo, A., Yang, Y., Park, G., McClean, J., and Mascareñas, D. (2021). A Holistic Cyber-physical Security Protocol for Authenticating the Provenance and Integrity of Structural

Health Monitoring Imagery Data. Structural Health Monitoring, 20(4), 1657–1674. doi:10.1177/1475921720927323

[15] Xu, Z., Liu, J., Lu, W., Xu, B., Zhao, X., Li, B., and Huang, J. (2021). Detecting Facial Manipulated Videos Based on Set Convolutional Neural Networks. Journal of Visual Communication Image Representation, 77 . doi:10.1016/j.jvcir.2021.103119

[16] Singh, G., Kumar, B., Gaur, L., and Tyagi, A. (2019). "Comparison between Multinomial and Bernoulli Naïve Bayes for Text Classification," 2019 International Conference on Automation, Computational and Technology Management (ICACTM), pp. 593–596. doi:10.1109/ICACTM.2019.8776800

[17] Gaur, L., Singh, G., Solanki, A., Jhanjhi, N. Z., Bhatia, U., Sharma, S., … and Kim, W. (2021). Disposition of Youth in Predicting Sustainable Development Goals Using the Neuro-fuzzy and Random Forest Algorithms. Human-Centric Computing and Information Sciences, 11, NA.

[18] Sharma, S., Singh, G., Gaur, L., and Sharma, R. (2022). Does Psychological Distance and Religiosity Influence Fraudulent Customer Behaviour? International Journal of Consumer Studies. doi:10.1111/ijcs.12773

[19] Sahu, G., Gaur, L., and Singh, G. (2021). Applying Niche and Gratification Theory Approach to Examine the Users' Indulgence Towards Over-the-Top Platforms and Conventional TV. Telematics and Informatics, 65 . doi:10.1016/j.tele.2021.101713

[20] Gaur, L., Ujjan, R.M.A. and Hussain, M., 2022. The Influence of Deep Learning in Detecting Cyber Attacks on E-Government Applications. In *Cybersecurity Measures for E-Government Frameworks* (pp. 107–122). IGI Global.

[21] Ramakrishnan, R., Gaur, L., and Singh, G. (2016). Feasibility and Efficacy of BLE Beacon IoT Devices in Inventory Management at the Shop Floor. International Journal of Electrical and Computer Engineering, 6(5), 2362–2368. doi:10.11591/ijece.v6i5.10807

[22] Afaq, A., Gaur, L., Singh, G., and Dhir, A. (2021). COVID-19: Transforming Air Passengers' Behaviour and Reshaping Their Expectations Towards the Airline Industry. Tourism Recreation Research. doi:10.1080/02508281.2021.2008211

[23] Gaur, L., Bhatia, U., Jhanjhi, N.Z., Muhammad, G. and Masud, M., (2021). Medical Image-Based Detection of COVID-19 Using Deep Convolution Neural Networks. Multimedia Systems, pp. 1–10.

[24] Anshu, K., Gaur, L. and Singh, G., (2022). Impact of Customer Experience on Attitude and Repurchase Intention in Online Grocery Retailing: A Moderation Mechanism of Value Co-creation. Journal of Retailing and Consumer Services, 64, p. 102798.

[25] Mahbub, M.K., Biswas, M., Gaur, L., Alenezi, F. and Santosh, K.C., (2022). Deep Features to Detect Pulmonary Abnormalities in Chest X-rays Due to Infectious DiseaseX: Covid-19, Pneumonia, and Tuberculosis. *Information Sciences*, 592, pp. 389–401.

[26] Gaur, L., Afaq, A., Solanki, A., Singh, G., Sharma, S., Jhanjhi, N.Z., My, H.T. and Le, D.N., (2021). Capitalizing on Big Data and Revolutionary 5G Technology: Extracting and Visualizing Ratings and Reviews of Global Chain Hotels. Computers & Electrical Engineering, 95, p. 107374.

[27] Anshu, K., Gaur, L. and Solanki, A., (2021). Impact of Chatbot in Transforming the Face of Retailing – An Empirical Model of Antecedents and Outcomes. Recent Advances in Computer Science and Communications (Formerly: Recent Patents on Computer Science), 14(3), pp. 774–787.

[28] Kaswan, K.S., Gaur, L., Dhatterwal, J.S. and Kumar, R., (2021). AI-based Natural Language Processing for the Generation of Meaningful Information Electronic Health

Record (her) Data. In *Advanced AI Techniques and Applications in Bioinformatics* (pp. 41–86). CRC Press.

[29] Gaur, L., Jhanjhi, N.Z., Bakshi, S. and Gupta, P., (2022), February. Analyzing Consequences of Artificial Intelligence on Jobs using Topic Modeling and Keyword Extraction. In *2022 2nd International Conference on Innovative Practices in Technology and Management (ICIPTM)* (Vol. 2, pp. 435–440). IEEE.

[30] Gaur, L., (2022). Internet of Things in Healthcare. In *Geospatial Data Science in Healthcare for Society 5.0* pp. 131–140. Springer, Singapore.

# 3 Deep Learning Techniques for Creation of DeepFakes

*Loveleen Gaur, Gursimar Kaur Arora, and Noor Zaman Jhanjhi*

## CONTENTS

## 3.1  INTRODUCTION

The neoteric advancement and improvement in Artificial Intelligence (AI) have given birth to DFs. This exponential growth has seen various complex functions performed by a single technique, especially in Machine Learning (ML). ML techniques are long in the tooth; it is viable to create state-of-the-art content, apart from general functions such as predicting. The algorithms to create the synthetic media utilize the algorithms of DL. DL, a subset of ML, works on the concept of unsupervised learning algorithm neural networks, also called artificial neural networks (ANNs).

A neural network functions like the neurons of our brain. They caught wind in the 1980s, but due to the lack of data and processing power, they couldn't be implemented until the recent developments. Similar to how an axon delivers the message to other neurons while the role of the dendritic tree is to collect input from the neurons, the neural network has a complex process with multiple layers of interconnected units. The layers are connected through synapses. Each unit has a certain weightage. Perceptron shares the signal to the activation function. The activation function helps to identify patterns in the multiplex data to give a correct output. It is the deciding

DOI: 10.1201/9781003231493-3

factor about what information should be transferred to the next neuron. The other type of neural network is a convolutional neural network (CNN), which has a wide application in computer vision for image processing and detection and has a considerable role in creating DFs, which is discussed in the next section.

The two main functions considered the most important in neural networks are loss and weight. In DFs, the neural network scores itself by comparing the generated output to input and updates the weights according to the scores. The neural networks check if the weights are added to the right director or not. They'll check this through the output generated after the adjustment of weights. This process continues until the loss value has decreased considerably. It is constantly improving itself, a meta-learning technique. This self-learning technique will help in creating and self-assessing the output of fakes.

The movement of progress in technology has have been back and forth. The advancement in generative modeling for detecting DFs would also pave the path to better creation methods. Recent reviews and research show that DFs is the other word for the severe problem, a compelling symptom of existing diseases [1]. However, the only difference here is that the symptom is worse than the disease. But what if this pushes those cracks to be filled and be a force of change [2]. Thus, this chapter will explore the research done and the techniques used to create DFs such as General Adversarial Network (GAN), Autoencoder, Face Swap, Image Animation, and so forth.

## 3.2  CHEAPFAKES VS. DEEPFAKES

Even though they both come under the umbrella term of audio-visual manipulation techniques, Cheapfakes are often muddled with DFs. Cheapfakes are "cheaply" produced, where cheaply refers to no advanced technology used for its generation. Cheapfakes are more threatening. It can be created quickly, with no high-end graphical card needed or a large dataset, costing nothing [3].

Cheapfakes can be produced by Photoshop, any software, applications (for example, Snapchat), or as simple as decreasing or increasing the speed through the inbuilt features of editing for cameras and videos. DFs are generated through the technology of AI and ML. Another manipulation technique is digital rotoscoping, like DFs, but requires manual outlining of features [4].

### 3.2.1  DEEP MODELING

The skeleton to create DFs starts with Autoencoder (encoder-decoder), a type of CNN and General Adversarial Network (GAN). This section will provide an introduction to these techniques and explain their work.

### 3.2.2  AUTOENCODER

Autoencoder is named so, as it takes an input, compresses it down to an encoder, and the resulting output is the regenerated input. To better understand the autoencoder, imagine a channel for the flow of variants and data that is narrow in between and wide on the ends. The image, say Image A on the left end of the encoder, is the input. Different algorithms have various hidden layers, which are being worked out. The first hidden layer will look at patches of pixels, rather than one pixel at a time, for example, a patch of 3 × 3, to identify essential features. The next hidden layer will follow a similar process, based on the matrix of pixels, called a window, formed by the former layer [5,6,7,8,9].

However, this network gets more profound, as there are multiple sheets of variants depending on the features, and each feature makes up one lamina. Multiple features result in multiple laminas, called the convolutional layer. Subsequently, this is further simplified through the pooling method. In this method, one has reached the deepest layer, where the features have been successfully extracted. It gives the property to CNN of being spatially invariant, as it is not receptive to the object's position. When the image reaches the pooling layer, there is no information about the features concerning the input image, and the initial pixel size is lost.

Considering the earlier example of autoencoder as a channel, from the broader space through various hidden layers, compression, and feature extraction comes the narrow space in between, i.e., the latent space (Figure 3.1). It contains all the required information for the model to reconstruct the input through the decoder. For instance, if the input image was a face, then the latent space would have information related to eyes, closed or open, the expression of the face, etc. The decoder constructs the output image with the defined features from the latent space. Autoencoders have the unsupervised methodology, as it compares the output to input and makes the modifications between layers until a similar or almost mirror-like image of input is formed. In DFs, the working of autoencoders goes one step further as there is one encoder and two decoders. In this case, the input will be two images, say Image 1 and Image 2. The purpose of having one encoder for two images is to retain the essential features of both images in the latent space, the bottleneck.

The purpose of the bottleneck is to give the model the ability to recreate rather than just returning the same value as input. The two decoders are trained separately to identify the standard features within both faces. Decoder 1 will learn to reconstruct the face of Image 1 from the noisy input. After completing the training phase, the testing phase will have the resultant as Image 1 with features of Image 2 and Image 2 with features of Image 1, a face-swapping technique. This technique does not limit to only image synthesis. With the usage of the appropriate algorithm, image-to-video synthesis is possible, where the output will be an image turned to a video, with the

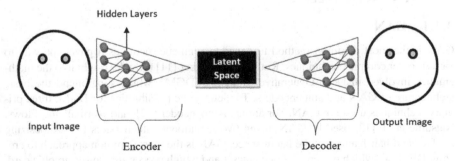

**FIGURE 3.1** Working of an autoencoder.

features and movement of the person in the video incorporated in the person in the image and video-to-video synthesis too, with certain limitations. To achieve a realistic and accurate output, the model needs to be trained on a large dataset, and the more complex the model, the better the outcome.

### 3.2.3 General Adversarial Network

While autoencoders are more accessible and easier to compute, GAN has produced more realistic results. In GAN, there are two neural networks, one being "Adversarial" on the other, to generate a synthesized output. It was introduced in the paper "General Adversarial Network" by Ian J. Goodfellow et al. [10], a dynamic idea to be proposed in the history of ML. The name GAN is derived from two fundamental techniques, the "Generative" method of deep learning, to make something new entirely on its own, which would be a reference result to the "Adversarial" technique that checks and compares the generated output to the input. The two neural networks are referred to as the generator and discriminator. The system of discriminators works on the principle of probability. The working is similar to that of the pendulum.

Consider the generator and discriminator on two opposite ends of the pendulum. The generator creates a new image attempts to trick the discriminator into passing the synthetic media as the real one. However, the discriminator network aims to estimate whether the image is computer-generated or real. Thus, in this way, the process moves back and forth, with the aim of the generator to let the discriminator make a mistake in establishing the probability. An ideal discriminator would make it extremely hard for the generator to create a realistic image, helping to produce a better output.

## 3.3 APPLICATIONS/SOFTWARES/PROGRAMS TO GENERATE DEEPFAKE

Table 3.1 presents an overview of the present application, software, and program available for use (free and paid) to create different types of DFs. It provides an array of models depending on the dataset, training team, and graphic card power.

## 3.4 DEEP DIVE INTO RELATED PAPERS TO GENERATE SYNTHETIC MEDIA

### 3.4.1 GAN

GAN is the most common method to generate synthetic media as it paves the way to various other complex techniques. Ruthotto and Haber [11] provide insight into the mathematics involved in Deep Generative Modeling (DGM), which superintend the basic architecture of GAN and autoencoders. To identify the possibilities for DGM, three primary techniques used are GAN, Variational Autoencoder [12], and Normalizing Flows. Natsume et al. [13] used RSGAN, using two variational autoencoders for synthesizing the face and hair features at the latent space. GAN is the most common approach to creating DFs [14], which requires a large dataset and a high processing power graphic card.

**TABLE 3.1**
**Different Types of Deep Fakes Models**

| Name | Models | Paid/Free | Type of DF |
|---|---|---|---|
| DFs web | Model based on face swap and loss value | Paid | Face swap |
| DeepFaceLab | H64, Avatar, SAE | Free | Face swap |
| Descript | ML-based model | Free trial/Paid version | Speech to text/ Audiogram |
| Doublicat | GAN/Reface | Free | Face swap, Gender swap |
| Deep Art Effects | GAN | The free and Paid version | Media into art |
| Deep Nostalgia by MyHeritage | Pre-set driving videos for image animation | Free trial/Paid Version | Image animation |
| FaceIt | GAN | Free | Face swap videos |
| Faceswap | Lightweight, Dfaker, Unbalanced, DFL-H128, DFL-SAE, Dlight, Realface | Free | Face swap |
| Face2Face | ML-based model | Free | Real-time facial re-enactment |
| FaceApp | GAN | The free and Paid version | Image manipulation |
| FSGAN (Face Swapping GAN) | Model based on RNN and Poisson blending loss | Free | Face swap and re-enactment |
| Generated Photos | StyleGAN | Free | Photo generation |
| Morphin | Image mapping | Free | Face mapping in gif media |
| Overdub | Descript/AI-based model | Free trial/Paid Version | Text-to-speech voice cloning/Audiograms |
| Reface | Model-based face embeddings | The free and Paid version | Celebrity Face swap |
| Reflect by NeoCortext | ML-based model | Free | Face swap |
| Tacotron 2 | Recurrent sequence to sequence feature prediction, WaveNet | Free | Speech synthesis from text |
| Wambo | Pre-set driving videos and motion capture, image mapping | Both Free & Paid version | Lip-Sync |
| WaveNet | CNN-based model | Free | Speech from text |
| Zao | AI-based model | Free | Face swap video |

Another technique to curb the obstacle of the enormous dataset has been researched by Zakharov et al. [15] by first training the algorithm (meta-training) with a large dataset. Then, the algorithm can generate a talking head DF with a few inputs only. Liu et al. [16] also explore various techniques to stabilize the GAN, such as stochastic gradient descent or ascent, etc. Another limitation to image generation through GAN is the vanishing gradient. To overcome this, Mao et al. [17] have proposed a Least Squares GAN model, in which the discriminator takes up the minor square loss function. For the generation of synthetic media, Cycle GAN uses two GAN networks. A unique framework, called MaskGAN, was introduced by Lee et al. [18], giving programmers the liberty and a better hand for DF creation to style copy and attribute transfer.

## 3.4.2 FACE SWAP

The face-swapping technique [19], though effective, has its limitations too. One of the ways to decipher this is through neural style transfer by using a trained CNN. Through style and structure transfer-based GAN [20], the authors from the 3D model create a 2D image by mapping on a stable surface. To receive a more realistic output for the style transfer method, Korshunova et al. [21] concocted an advanced loss function by addressing the limitations in previous research work by improving the face-swapping technique. Another obstacle to these novel DL algorithms such as GAN and variation autoencoder is creating a genuine-looking DF with clothes and a proper background. A probable solution can be training GAN on a spectral normalization technique [22], creating a new image in the wanted pose and background. And to overcome the problems faced during style transfer for face-swap technique, Guo et al. [23] have used an updated autoencoder technique. Natsume et al. [24] used FSNet architecture to produce face-swapped results.

Image-to-image translation [25] is older than DFs but has successfully created the synthetic media. This methodology of generating media is based on conditional adversarial networks [26], i.e., conditions of the output image are based on the input image. This technique is slightly different from the conventional working of GAN. The input for the discriminator is the source image, and the discriminator must identify if the target image has been created from the source image. An updated method was introduced by Lombardi et al. [27] to take in and encode the facial features and exhibit them in real-time, whereas Nirkin et al. [28] convolutional network for the replacement and face segmentation, by separately encoding the facial features of the source image and the target image, in the latent space.

## 3.4.3 AUDIO

Shimba et al. [29] have created talking heads, i.e., creating videos from synthesized audio by taking up the regression model and training it with Long Short-Term Memory (LSTM), whereas Santha [30] has used LSTM-based GAN to generate DFs. In Suwajanakorn et al. [31], the authors used the audio of Obama to create an optimum-quality video with perfect lip-sync to be added to a target video, using recurrent neural network (RNN). The model learned the audio notes and mouth movement with every passing frame by synthesizing the lower part of the face. This method has been updated, and audio to video is generated in real-time using Autoencoder and

CNN technique. Another CNN [6,7,8,9] is used to keep the quality of the video by maintaining sharp features [32].

Similarly, Prajwal et al. [33] fabricated a model with a trained discriminator focused on lip-sync; the output, using the audio clip, is a video with perfect lip-sync. Prajwal et al. [34] created a face video by taking input as image and audio and synthesizing LipGAN. In this framework, the role of the discriminator is to see if the face and audio are in synchronization. Another system introduced by Arik et al. [35] uses two approaches to synthesize and learn from a given voice, requiring only a few audio samples. The two approaches used are speaker encoding and speaker adoption. It is a neural voice cloning methodology. Another spectrum to explore in audio synthesis is speech-to-text synthesis, through Tacotron 2 [36], whose architecture is based on an updated model of WaveNet [37] and recurrent feature-to-feature prediction-based technique. The output is a human-like speech, where the model can be trained firsthand from the data. Following the method of voice cloning [38] is singing synthesis [39], by acquiring material for creating a multispeaker archetype. The authors aim to create a model that can train on the smaller dataset and adjust to new voices. The resultant voice had an optimum sound quality compared to the real one.

### 3.4.4 IMAGE ANIMATION

Face re-enactment is another type of face DF, apart from face swap, in which there is a source image and a target image, and the aim is to transfer the expression of the face in the source image to the target image. In this face re-enactment method [40,41], the authors have taken a target video and a source video recorded live through a webcam.

Forming the base of DF creation, Suwajanakorn et al. [42] created the puppeteer synthetic media, in which the video of Person B can control an image of Person A. Another dynamic advancement in creating DFs by Kim et al. [43] has used an input video to reanimate the portrait video. The limitation of this method was that the manipulation was limited to facial expressions only. However, the authors created DFs with whole head movement without any changes to the background or features of a person, such as hair/body.

With the advancement in research and technology [44,45,5], the authors of Siarohin et al. [46] have generated DF through image animation. They have used a source image and a driving video. Thus, two types of outputs are developed. First, the source image's face will be stable based on relative keypoint location, but the eyes and mouth movement would be like the driving video. Another one has a merged face of the input image and source video, and the face is moving too like the person in the video. It is a crucial point location, but the output, in this case, is slightly distorted. Balakrishnan et al. [47] used a generative neural network to manipulate images in unseen poses. The resultant has the same background but just a different pose. An adversarial discriminator was used to foresee that a realistic image is regenerated. Caporusso [48] has proposed a framework for an application for a three-way process (such as collecting data, processing phase, and finally the generation of synthetic content) to make it more accessible to users. It is used to gather data from the person at various stages of their lives and add it into an ML model to achieve an effective model to create Digital Twins.

To summarize the research done by the AI community, Table 3.2 provides an overview of the published study, techniques used, and the type of DF generated.

**TABLE 3.2**
**DeepFakes Model Adoption by Different Authors (Year-wise Comparison)**

| Author | Technique/Model | Year | DF |
|---|---|---|---|
| Metri and Mamatha [25] | GAN | 2021 | Image-to-image translation |
| Lanham [19] | GAN | 2021 | Face swapping |
| Liu et al. [16] | GAN | 2021 | Image and video synthesis |
| Kurupathi et al. [22] | Condition GAN | 2020 | Generating human images in different poses |
| Caporusso [48] | Three-way process application | 2020 | Digital twin |
| Siarohin et al. [46] | First-order motion model | 2020 | Image animation |
| Zhao and Chen [38] | Voice cloning | 2020 | Singing synthesis |
| Prajwal et al. [33] | GAN | 2020 | Lip-sync |
| Santha [30] | LSTM-based GAN | 2020 | DF |
| Lee et al. [15] | Mask GAN | 2020 | Facial image manipulation |
| Prajwal et al. [34] | Lip GAN | 2019 | Face video from an image and an audio |
| Blaauw et al. [39] | Multispeaker model | 2019 | Singing synthesis |
| Nirkin et al. [14] | FSGAN | 2019 | Face swapping and re-enactment |
| Zakharov et al. [15] | GAN | 2019 | Neural talking head model |
| Jamaludin et al. [32] | Autoencoder, CNN | 2019 | Audio-to-video synthesis |
| Balakrishnan et al. [47] | Generative neural network | 2018 | Recreating images of humans in unseen poses |
| Kim et al. [43] | AI | 2018 | Reanimate portrait video |
| Shen et al. [36] | Wavenet, Tacotron 2 | 2018 | Text-to-speech synthesis |
| Arik et al. [35] | Speaker encoder and speaker adoption | 2018 | Neural voice cloning |
| Nirkin et al. [28] | GAN | 2018 | Face segmentation and face swapping |
| Natsume et al. [24] | Fsnet | 2018 | Image-based face swapping |
| Guo et al. [23] | Style Transfer, Autoencoder | 2018 | Face swapping |
| Lombardi et al. [27] | CNN, Conditional Adversarial Network | 2018 | Facial image manipulation |
| Natsume et al. [13] | RSGAN | 2018 | Face swapping |
| Suwajanakorn et al. [31] | RNN | 2017 | Audio to lip-sync |
| Isola et al. [26] | Conditional Adversarial Network | 2017 | Image-to-image translation |
| Korshunova et al. [21] | Style transfer | 2017 | Face swapping |
| Thies et al. [40] | GAN | 2016 | Face re-enactment |
| Wang et al. [20] | Style and structure transfer-based GAN | 2016 | Face swapping |
| Suwajanakorn [42] | Autoencoder | 2015 | Puppeteer synthetic media |
| Thies et al. [41] | GAN | 2015 | Facial re-enactment |
| Shimba et al. [29] | LSTM, Regression model | 2015 | Creating a video from audio synthesis |

## 3.5 SUMMARY

DFs are synthetic media generated through meta-learning algorithms of ML and DL. This chapter read about the two algorithms that form the skeleton to form the DFs: Autoencoder and GAN. Few applications, software, and programs were enlisted with trained algorithms for the new users or those of non-technical background. Thorough research was done on the related papers and the techniques used by the researchers. The associated articles are broadly divided based on GAN, Face swap, audio synthesis, and image animation. Our research concluded that the limitation still exists about the training of the model quality of the dataset or the time taken to train the model. Thus, future research needs to focus on these aspects for an easier, faster, and a more realistic generation of DFs.

The next chapter will focus on the use of face warping artifacts to distinguish DF videos from the real ones effectively.

## REFERENCES

[1] Brownlee, J. (2019). How to Develop a Pix2Pix GAN for Image-to-Image Translation. https://machinelearningmastery.com/how-to-develop-a-pix2pix-gan-for-image-to-image-translation/, Positive uses of DFs (Article).

[2] Kietzmann, J., Lee, L. W., McCarthy, I. P., & Kietzmann, T. C. (2020). DFs: Trick or treat? Business Horizons, 63(2), 135–146. https://doi.org/10.1016/j.bushor.2019.11.006

[3] Loukides, M. (2021, May 11). DeepCheapFakes. O'Reilly Media. www.oreilly.com/radar/deepcheapfakes/ (Article).

[4] Paris, B., & Donovan, J. (2019, September 18). DFs and Cheap Fakes. Data & Society. https://datasociety.net/library/DFs-and-cheap-fakes/. Harvard Kennedy School Report.

[5] Gaur, L., Afaq, A., Singh, G. & Dwivedi, Y. K. (2021). Role of artificial intelligence and robotics to foster the touchless travel during a pandemic: A review and research agenda. International Journal of Contemporary Hospitality Management, 33(11), 4079–4098. https://doi.org/10.1108/IJCHM-11-2020-1246

[6] Singh, G., Kumar, B., Gaur, L., & Tyagi, A. (2019). "Comparison between Multinomial and Bernoulli Naïve Bayes for Text Classification," *2019 International Conference on Automation, Computational and Technology Management (ICACTM)*, pp. 593–596. doi:10.1109/ICACTM.2019.8776800.

[7] Gaur, L., Singh, G., Solanki, A., Jhanjhi, N. Z., Bhatia, U., Sharma, S., ... & Kim, W. (2021), "Disposition of youth in predicting sustainable development goals using the neuro-fuzzy and random forest algorithms" Human-Centric Computing and Information Sciences, 11, NA.

[8] Rana, J., Gaur, L., Singh, G., Awan, U. & Rasheed, M. I. (2021). Reinforcing customer journey through artificial intelligence: A review and research agenda. International Journal of Emerging Markets, Vol. ahead-of-print (No. ahead-of-print). https://doi.org/10.1108/IJOEM-08-2021-1214

[9] Sharma, D. K., Gaur, L., & Okunbor, D. (2007). Image compression and feature extraction with neural network. Proceedings of the Academy of Information and Management Sciences, 11(1), 33–38.

[10] Goodfellow, I., Pouget-Abadie, J., Mirza, M., Xu, B., Warde-Farley, D., Ozair, S., Courville, A., & Bengio, Y. (2014). GANs. Communications of the ACM, 63(11), 139–144. https://doi.org/10.1145/3422622

[11] Ruthotto, L., & Haber, E. (2021). An introduction to deep generative modeling. GAMM-Mitteilungen, 44(2). https://doi.org/10.1002/gamm.202100008

[12] Pinheiro Cinelli, L., Araújo Marins, M., Barros da Silva, E. A., & Lima Netto, S. (2021). Variational autoencoder. Variational Methods for ML with Applications to Deep Networks, 111–149. Springer. https://doi.org/10.1007/978-3-030-70679-1_5

[13] Natsume, R., Yatagawa, T., & Morishima, S. (2018). "Rsgan: Face swapping and editing using face and hair representation in latent spaces," arXiv preprint arXiv:1804.03447. https://doi.org/10.1145/3230744.3230818

[14] Nirkin, Y., Keller, Y., & Hassner, T. (2019). "FSGAN: Subject agnostic face swapping and reenactment," in Proceedings of the IEEE International Conference on Computer Vision, pp. 7184–7193 https://doi.org/10.1109/ICCV.2019.00728

[15] Zakharov, E., Shysheya, A., Burkov, E., & Lempitsky, V. (2019). Few-shot adversarial learning of realistic neural talking head models. 2019 IEEE/CVF International Conference on Computer Vision (ICCV). https://doi.org/10.1109/iccv.2019.00955

[16] Liu, M.-Y., Huang, X., Yu, J., Wang, T.-C., & Mallya, A. (2021). GANs for image and video synthesis: Algorithms and applications. Proceedings of the IEEE, 1–24. https://doi.org/10.1109/jproc.2021.3049196

[17] Mao, X., Li, Q., Xie H., Lau R., Zhen W., & Smolley, S. (2017). Least Squares GANs. https://doi.org/10.1109/ICCV.2017.304

[18] Lee, C.-H., Liu, Z., Wu, L., & Luo, P. (2020). Maskgan: Towards diverse and interactive facial image manipulation. 2020 IEEE/CVF Conference on Computer Vision and Pattern Recognition (CVPR). https://doi.org/10.1109/cvpr42600.2020.00559

[19] Lanham, M. (2021). DFs and face-swapping. Generating a New Reality, 255–285. Springer. https://doi.org/10.1007/978-1-4842-7092-9_9

[20] Wang, X., & Gupta, A. (2016). Generative image modelling using style and structure adversarial networks. In European Conference on Computer Vision, pp. 318–335. Springer. https://doi.org 10.1007/978-3-319-46493-0_20

[21] Korshunova, I., Shi, W., Dambre, J., & Theis, L. (2017). Fast Face-Swap using convolutional neural networks. 2017 IEEE International Conference on Computer Vision (ICCV). https://doi.org/10.1109/iccv.2017.397

[22] Kurupathi, S., Murthy, P., & Stricker, D. (2020). Generation of human images with clothing using advanced conditional GANs. Proceedings of the 1st International Conference on DL Theory and Applications. https://doi.org/10.5220/0009832200300041

[23] Guo, Y., He, W., Zhu, J., & Li, C. (2018). A light autoencoder network for face swapping. Proceedings of the 2018 2nd International Conference on Computer Science and AI- CSAI '18. https://doi.org/10.1145/3297156.3297210

[24] Natsume, R., Yatagawa, T., & Morishima, S. (2018). "Fsnet: An identity-aware generative model for image-based face swapping," in Asian Conference on Computer Vision, pp. 117–132. Springer. https://doi.org/10.1007/978-3-030-20876-9_8

[25] Metri, O., & Mamatha, H. R. (2021). Image generation using GANs. GANs for Image-to-Image Translation, 235–262. Elsevier. https://doi.org/10.1016/b978-0-12-823519-5.00007-5

[26] Isola, P., Zhu, J.-Y., Zhou, T., & Efros, A. A. (2017). Image-to-image translation with conditional adversarial networks. 2017 IEEE Conference on Computer Vision and Pattern Recognition (CVPR). https://doi.org/10.1109/cvpr.2017.632

[27] Lombardi, S., Saragih, J., Simon, T., & Sheikh, Y. (2018). Deep appearance models for face rendering. ACM Transactions on Graphics, 37(4), 1–13. https://doi.org/10.1145/3197517.3201401

[28] Nirkin, Y., Masi, I., Tuan, A. T., Hassner, T., & Medioni, G. (2018). "On face segmentation, face swapping, and face perception," in 2018 13th IEEE International Conference on Automatic Face & Gesture Recognition (FG 2018), pp. 98–105: IEEE. https://doi.org/10.1109/FG.2018.00024

[29] Shimba, T., Sakurai, R., Yamazoe, H., & Lee, J.-H. (2015). Talking heads synthesis from audio with deep neural networks. 2015 IEEE/SICE International Symposium on System Integration (SII). https://doi.org/10.1109/sii.2015.7404961 FaceSwap GAN: https://github.com/shaoanlu/faceswap-GAN

[30] Santha, A. (2020). DFs generation Using LSTM Based GANs (theses). Rochester Institute of Technology. Accessed from https://scholarworks.rit.edu/theses/10447

[31] Suwajanakorn, S., Seitz, S. M., & Kemelmacher-Shlizerman, I. (2017). Synthesizing Obama: Learning lip sync from audio. ACM Transactions on Graphics, 36(4), Article 95. https://doi.org/10.1145/3072959.3073640

[32] Jamaludin, A., Chung, J. S., & Zisserman, A. (2019). You said that? Synthesizing talking faces from audio. International Journal of Computer Vision, 127(11–12), 1767–1779. https://doi.org/10.1007/s11263-019-01150-y

[33] Prajwal, K. R., Mukhopadhyay, R., Namboodiri, V. P., & Jawahar, C. V. (2020). A lip sync expert is all you need for speech to lip generation in the wild. Proceedings of the 28th ACM International Conference on Multimedia. https://doi.org/10.1145/3394171.3413532

[34] Prajwal, K. R., Mukhopadhyay, R., Philip, J., Jha, A., Namboodiri, V., & Jawahar, C. V. (2019). Towards automatic face-to-face translation. Proceedings of the 27th ACM International Conference on Multimedia. https://doi.org/10.1145/3343031.3351066

[35] Arik, S., Chen, J., Peng, K., Ping, W., & Zhou, Y. (2018). "Neural voice cloning with a few samples," in Advances in Neural Information Processing Systems, pp. 10019–10029.

[36] Shen, J., Pang, R., Weiss, R. J., Schuster, M., Jaitly, N., Yang, Z., ... Wu, Y. (2018). Natural TTS Synthesis by Conditioning Wavenet on MEL Spectrogram Predictions. 2018 IEEE International Conference on Acoustics, Speech and Signal Processing (ICASSP). doi:10.1109/icassp.2018.8461368

[37] WaveNet: A generative model for raw audio. Deepmind. (n.d.). https://deepmind.com/blog/article/wavenet-generative-model-raw-audio.

[38] Zhao, L., & Chen, F. "Research on Voice Cloning with a Few Samples," 2020 International Conference on Computer Network, Electronic and Automation (ICCNEA), 2020, pp. 323–328. https://doi.org/10.1109/ICCNEA50255.2020.00073.

[39] Blaauw, M., Bonada, J., & Daido, R. (2019). Data efficient voice cloning for neural singing synthesis. ICASSP 2019–2019 IEEE International Conference on Acoustics, Speech and Signal Processing (ICASSP). https://doi.org/10.1109/icassp.2019.8682656

[40] Thies, J., Zollhofer, M., Stamminger, M., Theobalt, C., & Niessner, M. (2016). Face2Face: Real-time face capture and reenactment of RGB videos. 2016 IEEE Conference on Computer Vision and Pattern Recognition (CVPR). https://doi.org/10.1109/cvpr.2016.262

[41] Thies, J., Zollhöfer, M., Nießner, M., Valgaerts, L., Stamminger, M., & Theobalt, C. (2015). Real-time expression transfer for facial reenactment. ACM Transactions on Graphics, 34(6), 1–14. https://doi.org/10.1145/2816795.2818056

[42] Suwajanakorn, S., Seitz, S. M., & Kemelmacher-Shlizerman, I. (2015). What makes Tom Hanks look Like Tom Hanks. 2015 IEEE International Conference on Computer Vision (ICCV). https://doi.org/10.1109/iccv.2015.450

[43] Kim, H., Garrido, P., Tewari, A., Xu, W., Thies, J., Nießner, M., Pérez, P., Richardt, C., Zollhöfer, M., & Theobalt, C. (2018). Deep Video Portraits. https://doi.org/10.1145/ 3197517.3201283

[44] Gaur, L., Afaq, A., Solanki, A., Singh, G., Sharma, S., Jhanjhi, N. Z., … Le, D. (2021). Capitalizing on big data and revolutionary 5G technology: Extracting and visualizing ratings and reviews of global chain hotels. Computers and Electrical Engineering, 95. doi:10.1016/j.compeleceng.2021.107374

[45] Gaur, L., Bhatia, U., Jhanjhi, N. Z., Muhammad, G., & Masud, M. (2021). Medical image-based detection of COVID-19 using deep convolution neural networks. Multimedia Systems. doi:10.1007/s00530-021-00794-6

[46] Siarohin, A., Lathuilière, S., Tulyakov, S., Ricci, E., & Sebe, N. (2020). First Order Motion Model for Image Animation. Part of Advances in Neural Information Processing Systems 32 (NeurIPS 2019).

[47] Balakrishnan, G., Zhao, A., Dalca, A. V., Durand, F., & Guttag, J. (2018). Synthesizing images of humans in unseen poses. 2018 IEEE/CVF Conference on Computer Vision and Pattern Recognition. https://doi.org/10.1109/cvpr.2018.00870

[48] Caporusso, N. (2020). DFs for The good: A beneficial application of contentious AI technology. Advances in Intelligent Systems and Computing, 235–241. Springer USA. https://doi.org/10.1007/978-3-030-51328-3_33

# 4 Analyzing DeepFakes Videos by Face Warping Artifacts

*Ajantha Devi Vairamani*

## CONTENTS

DOI: 10.1201/9781003231493-4

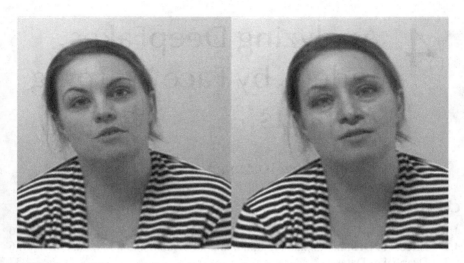

**FIGURE 4.1**    A DF-created picture (right) based on an individual (left).

## 4.1   INTRODUCTION

DeepFakes (DFs) mix the words "Deep learning" and "fake." DFs is an innovation that superimposes the objective individual's facial picture on the source individual's video, as shown in Figure 4.1, causing the objective individual to have all the earmarks of playing out similar exercises as the source individual in the video. Models such as Autoencoders and General Adversarial Network (GAN) are often utilized in PC vision to deal with picture division, face acknowledgment, and multi-view facial picture amalgamation issues. DFs calculations are also used to look at an individual's facial feelings and developments, just as facial picture amalgamation of someone else, making tantamount articulations and developments [1].

DFs innovation was proposed interestingly toward the finish of 2017. In light of the Encoder-Decoder system, GAN innovation was dispatched to present DFs innovation. Utilizing the advancement guideline of the game hypothesis, the GAN calculation not just lessens the number of model boundaries and model intricacy under similar conditions but also makes the produced face amazingly sensible, thus diminishing the dependence on the first photograph and working on the impact of the evolving faces, in any event, confusing the deceptive one with the authentic one [2].

## 4.2   EFFECTS OF DFS

DFs is the quickest developing Artificial Intelligence (AI) innovation [3] that acquired the reputation of its use in the production of deep recordings. For instance, specific individuals utilize this innovation to create obscene substance or fake government official discourses and other things. Honestly, as well as influencing the video's validness, DFs innovation may be utilized to manufacture proof. For instance, cheats can make counterfeit motion pictures concerning its chiefs' mischief to threaten and

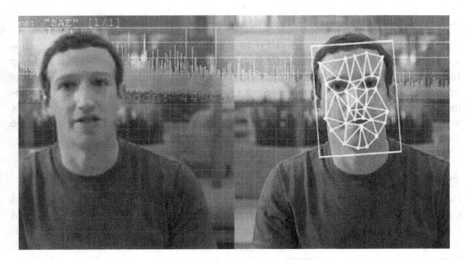

**FIGURE 4.2**  The devastating effect of a DF has raised many concerns and has hit Indian shores (Picture: CNBC).

coerce a partnership. More regrettable, the spread of DFs innovation-created recordings has prompted the colossal outcome that nobody accepts the genuine recordings [4,5].

DFs, then again, offer a few benefits; for example, helping people who have lost their voices in making commotions or refreshing film cuts without re-recording [1]. Driving individuals, just as refined PC frameworks, are experiencing issues spotting fake photographs and recordings as shown in Figure 4.2 as cutting-edge deep neural networks (DNNs) improve and a colossal measure of information opens up [6]. Delivering fake pictures and movies is turning out to be progressively simpler nowadays, and everything necessary is a character photograph or a brief video from the objective individual. Thus, DFs affect both people of note and customary people [7]. The voice of the CEO of a British energy company's German parent firm cheated numerous associates and accomplices for 220,000 Euros in only one day [8]. One more episode happened on utilizing AI to make a DF image and a profile on LinkedIn, deceiving various individuals, including the government authorities [9].

## 4.3  DEEPFAKES DATASETS

As a result of DFs' abuse and the rapid evolution, studying DFs detection methods has become increasingly complex. The availability of the DFs large-scale dataset is a critical component in the advancement of DFs detection algorithms.

### 4.3.1  UADFV

The UADFV dataset [10] was one of the first public databases to detect DFs. There are 49 real YouTube videos in the database. These films are utilized to make 49 forgeries videos for the target face using FakeApp mobile devices.

### 4.3.2 DEEPFAKES-TIMIT (DF-TIMIT)

The University of Queensland (UQ) in Australia created the Vid-TIMIT audio-video dataset [11]. The other dataset is the DFs-TIMIT dataset from the Swiss Idiap Institute, which is organized using the Vid-TIMIT dataset [12]. Each of the 43 objects in the Vid-TIMIT database has screened 13 real videos. The DF-TIMIT dataset contains 32 themes and 620 DFs videos from the Vid-TIMIT dataset. Faceswap-GAN was used to make these synthesized videos. There are 10,537 actual photos in the dataset and 34,023 synthetic images generated from 320 videos.

### 4.3.3 FACEFORENSICS ++

FaceForensics ++ [13] is a face-forged dataset that investigators may use to train supervised deep learning-based methods. DFs, Face2Face, NeuralTextures, and FaceSwap are four automatic facial manipulation techniques used to change 1,000 starting video sequences. These figures is based on YouTube 977 videos, all of which have traceable and predominantly front-side faces with no cover, allowing for realistic forgeries to be created using automated tampering methods.

### 4.3.4 GOOGLE DEEPFAKES DETECTION—DFD

Google Research created the DF Detection (DFD) dataset [14] by recording 100 videos in 28 different scenarios with paid and volunteer actors. Then, using the freely accessible DFs production method, more than 3,000 DFs were created from these videos. The DFD dataset, which includes natural and false videos, detects DFs.

### 4.3.5 FACEBOOK DEEPFAKES DETECTION CHALLENGE—DFDC

Facebook gathered and produced the DF Detection Challenge (DFDC) dataset [15], including 5K videos with two face modification algorithms. Facebook engages a team of professional actors to capture various deep bionic technologies. Each participant had to submit a set of movies to execute a set of predetermined tasks. These movies include a variety of lighting situations, head stances, and diversity of axes (gender, skin color, and age).

### 4.3.6 CELEB-DF

The Celeb-DF-v1 dataset [16] contains real and DFs composite videos of comparable quality to those found on the internet. The Celeb-DF dataset includes 408 actual YouTube videos of various genders, ages, and races, as well as 795 DFs made from these recordings.

Actual and DFs composite videos with video quality comparable to internet diffusion videos are included in the Celeb-DF-v2 dataset [17]. The Celeb-DF-v2 dataset is substantially more significant than the previous Celeb-DF-v1 dataset, which contained just 795 DFs. Celeb-DF now has 590 YouTube videos with various ethnicities, genders, ages, and celebrities.

## 4.4 DFS DETECTION

One of the most well-known artistic creations of Abraham Lincoln, the U.S. President, dating from around 1865, contains the soonest recorded endeavor at face trading. As displayed in Figure 4.3, the lithography joins the head of Abraham Lincoln and the body of Southern pioneer John Calhoun. Following Lincoln's death, his lithographies were popular, and inscriptions of his head on various bodies showed up practically short-term [18].

As demonstrated in Figure 4.4, DFs detection techniques are isolated into two classifications: fake picture detection and fake video detection. The justification behind this grouping is that, because of the critical weakening created by video pressure, most picture identification procedures cannot be straightforwardly used for video location. Besides, recordings incorporate planning qualities that change with various casings, making static picture recognition methods testing to recognize [19].

Ongoing upgrades in the picture and video altering [20,21] have radically changed the battleground. The democratization of present-day advancements has sped up this worldview change, for example, TensorFlow [22] and Keras [23], just as open admittance to late specialized writing and minimal expense register gear. They are altering photos and recordings, which were already simply accessible to exceptionally prepared subject matter experts as in Figure 4.5, utilizing convolutional autoencoders [19,24] and GAN [25,26] models. Cell phone and PC applications dependent on this method incorporate FaceApp [27] and FakeApp [28].

**FIGURE 4.3** Face moving: The government official John Calhoun was traded with U.S. President Abraham Lincoln (left). The head of Jimmy Fallon and John Oliver were exchanged in FakeApp (right) [28].

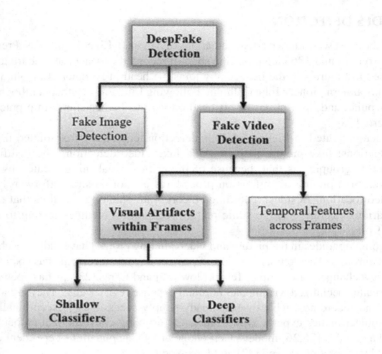

**FIGURE 4.4**    The classification of DFs detection methods.

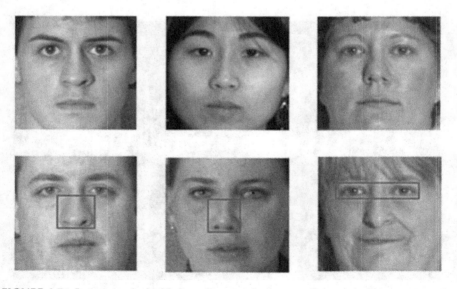

**FIGURE 4.5**    Images marked with the red rectangular box are the tampered images.

FaceApp is a program that mechanizes the age of photograph practical facial adjustments. You can change your face, hairdo, age, sexual orientation, and different provisions with your cell phone. FakeApp is an application that permits the clients to produce "DFs" recordings.

Although some DF videos are innocuous, they are in the minority. Up until this point, DF video advancements [28] have been used to counterfeit big-name obscene recordings and vengeance pornography [29]. On stages such as Reddit, Twitter, and Pornhub, this kind of porn is now precluded. DF recordings are an objective for Ped sexual material, counterfeit reconnaissance film, fake news, and other terrible substances due to their exact nature. Government organizations are seriously viewing these fake motion pictures, which have recently been utilized to kindle political strains [30].

## 4.5 METHODS OF FACE-BASED VIDEO MANIPULATION

A few methods for perceiving facial modifications in video groupings were developed during the 1990s [31,32]. Thies et al. were quick to accomplish constant appearance moves for faces. They later presented Face2Face [19], a consistent facial reenactment framework that can alter face developments across different videos. Options in contrast to Face2Face have additionally been introduced [33]. The scientists [34] indicated that a few deep learning-based face picture age calculations have likewise been analyzed. GANs have been utilized to age faces [26] and modify facial attributes such as skin tone [35].

Deep feature interpolation [33] produces stunning outcomes regarding changing facial features such as age, beard growth, and mouthfeel. Lample et al. [34] get comparable discoveries with property additions. The picture goal of most DL-based picture combination calculations is unobtrusive. Karras et al. [35] show excellent face blend utilizing moderate GANs to develop picture quality further.

Recurrent Neural Networks (RNNs), as in Figure 4.6, is a kind of neural network that continues to rehash the same thing. Long Short-Term Memory (LSTM) networks were explored by Hochreiter and Schmidhuber [36] as a kind of RNN [37] for learning long haul conditions in input arrangements. DL models utilizing both an LSTM and a convolutional neural network (CNN) are alluded to as "somewhere down in space" and "somewhere down on schedule," which are two different framework modalities.

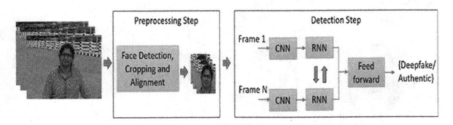

**FIGURE 4.6** Face manipulation detection using RNN.

### 4.5.1 Temporal Features Across Frames

Temporal features across outlines make choices dependent on time-related properties in a video, like human flicker recurrence and mouth shape, ordinarily utilizing recursive characterization strategies.

#### 4.5.1.1  Using Recurrent Neural Networks

The start to finish framework is explored by specialists [38]. The earlier CNN network utilizes ImageNet to prepare the InceptionV3 model ahead of time [39,40] during the given video succession. Still, it will erase a final, connected layer to construct a 2048-dimensional trademark vector for each casing. The LSTM network gets the trademark vector as info. The probability of validness and fake is at long last processed utilizing softmax, as shown in Figure 4.7, after the 512-dimensional associated layer.

The specialists tried different things with movies of different casing spans after gathering 300 DFs recordings from the site. We can see from the outcomes that this calculation can precisely foresee whether a broken-down section is from a deeply created video in under two seconds of a video (40 edges of the video are inspected at 24 casings each second) with an exactness pace up to 97%. Notwithstanding, it has the disadvantage of requiring both genuine and bogus pictures as preparing information, making it wasteful.

#### 4.5.1.2  Eye Blinking

The blinking recurrence [41,42] of the video face location identifies shut eyelids in the preparation tests dependent on the DFs engineered video. To start, distinguish each edge's face, find the facial region, and concentrate fundamental provisions from the face, such as the tip of the eyes, the lips, the nose, and the shapes of the cheeks. Then, use the milestones-based face arrangement strategy to adjust a face region into the uniform organized space, keeping away from impedance brought about by changes in head development and face direction in video outlines. Then, at that point, to set up a consistent arrangement, find and eliminate the natural eye and send it to the Long-term Recurrent Convolutional Networks (LRCN) network.

LRCN network: to decide the condition of the eye, first concentrate natural eye highlights utilizing VGG16 [43], as in Figure 4.8, then, at that point, input RNN and LSTM units, and then, at that point, send the yield to the completely associated layer,

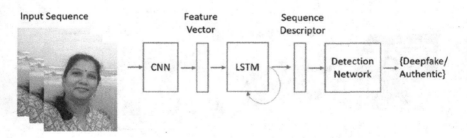

**FIGURE 4.7**   A DF detection method using a convolutional neural network (CNN).

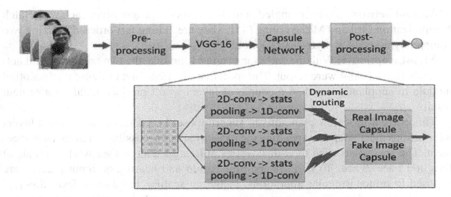

**FIGURE 4.8** Deep features obtained from the VGG-16 network.

which works out the likelihood of open or shut eyes. At long last, train the CNN network, LSTM-RNN, and completely associated layers exclusively utilizing the two-class characterization cross-entropy misfortune work.

In a test, the scientists substitute the LRCN technique [44] with a VGG16 two-class grouping network and an eye angle proportion (EAR)-based system. Subsequently, when contrasted with CNN 0.98 and EAR 0.79, LRCN has the best exhibition (0.99) as far as the district under ROC (AUC). At last, the actual video has a flickering recurrence of 34:1/min. In contrast, the deep video has 3.4/min squints, so I set an ordinary individual's flickering recurrence edge of 10/min. We can determine if this video is fake.

## 4.5.2 VISUAL ARTIFACTS INSIDE FRAMES

The investigation of visual antiques inside the casing is tended to in this segment, which uses imperfections on the picture's edge just as unnatural subtleties such as facial elements and facial shadows to assess, remove explicit qualities, and finish the discovery with deep or shallow classifiers. The components are then isolated into superficial or deep classifiers, separating genuine and counterfeit recordings.

### 4.5.2.1 Deep Classifiers

Since the goal of DFs recordings is constantly restricted, we should utilize the relative surface contortion strategy (for example, scaling, pivot, and cutting). Since the twisted face parts don't coordinate with the general climate, a deep shadow is made, which the CNN model can recognize. We should view the connected recognition techniques dependent on the deep classifier next.

Miniature examination dependent on picture commotion, for instance, won't work in compacted video circumstances where picture clamor should be diminished. Also, imitations photographs [45] are hard to identify with the unaided eye at a more elevated level of semantics, particularly when an image portrays the human face. Thus, the scientists suggested a transitional technique for a DNN with a predetermined number of layers.

**Meso-4 network** has four tangled neural networks in progression, each with Batch Normalization [46] and Max Pooling [47]. They are at long last ordered utilizing two completely associated layers and sigmoid.

**MesoInception-4:** With the variation origin v1 module, the two tangled neural networks before Meso-4 were re-put. The specialist mentions that utilizing the Inception module to supplant more than a couple of layers won't produce ideal arrangement results.

This current module's plan aims to superimpose the yields of two tangled layers with various piece shapes, expanding the capacity space accessible for model advancement. The specialists tried their discoveries utilizing a dataset they worked on about DFs and Face-2Face. To build oversimplification and heartiness, input patches are exposed to minor irregular alterations, including scaling, revolution, level flipping, and brilliance and shading changes. Under natural network dispersion conditions, the normal discovery pace of this methodology for DFs video is 90%, and the normal recognition pace of Face2Face video is 95%.

### 4.5.2.1.1   Face Warping Artifacts

This methodology depends on the characteristics in Figure 4.9 of the DFs video [48]. Because of an absence of creation time and computational assets, the DFs technique can amalgamate low-goal face pictures, which should go through a relative change to coordinate with the source face arrangement. Since the goals of the twisted surface area and its quick encompasses are conflicting, this bending brings about particular deep shadows in the DFs video, which customary DNN models can effectively catch (such as VGG, ResNet [49], etc.).

Advantages: Using negative samples as training data is a simple picture processing operation, which saves computational time and resources.

Disadvantages: Overfitting the DFs video with a specific distribution is possible.

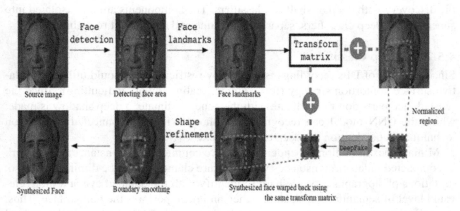

**FIGURE 4.9**   Overview of the DF production pipeline.

#### 4.5.2.2  Shallow Classifiers

Shallow classifiers necessitate a feature extractor capable of resolving perfection's selectivity–invariance problem. One helpful feature extractor can generate a single feature; that is, it can extract valuable information for recognizing the picture's content while discarding unnecessary data such as the animal's position. The previous section covered deep classifiers, and this section will cover shallow classifier-based related methods.

##### 4.5.2.2.1  Using Inconsistent Head Poses

DFs are created by sewing the generated face area into the original photograph. It will introduce mistakes when calculating a three-dimensional head posture (such as head direction and location) from a two-dimensional facial image. Researchers use the Support Vector Machine (SVM) classifier [50] to classify this feature and undertake experiments to prove the phenomena. Researchers compared estimated head postures based on whole-facial coordinate points, with head poses simply on the center face area, finding that they are highly comparable in the actual face.

The specialists consider the head course vector to improve the issue, acquiring two-head three-dimensional unit vectors determined from the entire face and the middle face and contrasting cosine distances.

The cosine distance of a few head position vectors determined from natural appearances is centered around a restricted reach (up to 0.02). DFs' two vector cosine distance esteems, then again, are scattered in the scope of 0.02–0.08, demonstrating that they can be separated from one another along these lines. The SVM classifier was additionally prepared in the UADDV dataset [51] and the DARPA GAN Challenge dataset [52].

##### 4.5.2.3  DeepFakes and Face Manipulations

Unique fake visual artifacts [53,54] can be made using existing video production algorithms. These characteristics are discernible by inspecting the eyes, teeth, and face contours. Researchers classify these manufactured visual artifacts into the following categories:

Global consistency: The term "global consistency" refers to the inconsistency of the color of the iris in the left and right eyes. Heterochromia is reasonably rare in reality, but the degree of this occurrence in the generated face varies greatly, as illustrated in Figure 4.10.

Illumination estimation: While the Face2face procedure [55] explicitly utilizes enlightenment assessment, mathematical assessment, and delivering examples to demonstrate, the error or wrong evaluation of episode light is probably going to initiate relating relics in the face made by deep learning. This antique often creates in the space encompassing the nose, for instance, making one side surprisingly dull. Also, the specular appearance in the eyes is either lost or rearranged by deep learning, as shown in Figures 4.10 and 4.11.

Geometry estimation: Wrong mathematical assessment of the human face causes clear limits, just as high-contrast counterfeit antiques, to show up on the restrictions of the human face and cover. Besides, to some extent, hindered facial portion, such

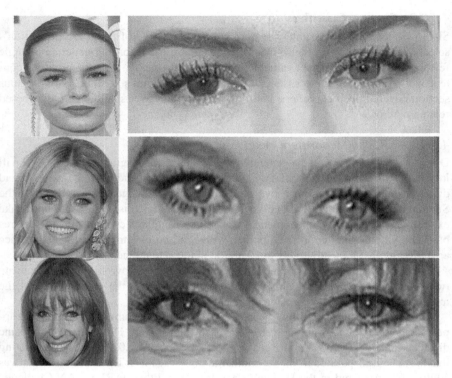

**FIGURE 4.10** Global consistency and illumination estimation errors.

**FIGURE 4.11** Illumination estimation and geometric estimation errors.

**FIGURE 4.12**   Geometric estimation errors.

as an inappropriate haircut, will bring about "emptiness." Furthermore, teeth are now and again not portrayed by any means, as found in a few movies. Teeth show up in these films as little white spots instead of individual teeth, as illustrated in Figures 4.11 and 4.12.

By separating these components to build highlight vector gatherings, the specialists look to prepare KNN [56], MLP [57], strategic relapse model [58], and different classifiers on the full-face produced by GAN, DFs, and Face2face information. Since highlights characterize specific counterfeit items, these little classifiers can likewise perform order undertakings dependent on the outcomes. It is also a critical benefit of this procedure over others that utilize deep classifiers to prepare information and time, regardless of whether the result isn't extraordinary.

## 4.6   DIFFICULTIES IN DETECTING DEEPFAKES

Although critical advancement has been accomplished in the exhibition of DF locators, there are various issues with present identification calculations. This segment examines a portion of the challenges that DF location procedures face, as shown in Figure 4.13.

**FIGURE 4.13** Dataset comparison.

### 4.6.1 DeepFake Datasets' Quality

The capacity to get to substantial information bases of DFs is a vital viewpoint in improving DF location calculations. Nonetheless, contrasting the nature of recordings from these datasets to real altered substance appropriated on the web uncovered huge inconsistencies. The accompanying visual curios can be found in these information bases:

i.    worldly gleaming during discourse,
ii.   haziness around the facial areas,
iii.  over perfection in facial surface/absence of facial surface subtleties,
iv.   absence of the head presents development or revolution,
v.    absence of impending face articles such as glasses, lightning impact, and so forth
vi.   touchy to changes in input stance or look, irregularity in complexion, and character leakage
vii.  limited accessibility of a joined top-notch general media DF dataset. The ambiguities in the dataset demonstrated earlier are because of mistakes in the control methods.

Besides, the adjusted bad-quality substances can be hard to convince or establish a certified connection. Thus, regardless of whether discovery frameworks beat such recordings, there is no assurance that these techniques will do well in reality. Furthermore, modified low-quality content can be difficult to persuade or make a genuine impression. As a result, even if detection systems outperform such videos, there is no guarantee that these methods will do well in the real world.

### 4.6.2 Evaluation of Performance

DF location calculations are now expressed as a similar characterization issue, in which each example may be genuine or counterfeit. Such order is simpler to create in a controlled setting, where we develop and test DF identification frameworks utilizing either real or produced available media content. Nonetheless, in genuine conditions, movies can be modified in manners other than DFs; consequently, the film that hasn't been found as controlled isn't generally bona fide.

Besides, because DF content can be changed in various ways, like general media, a solitary name may not be thoroughly right. Moreover, at least one individual's appearance is typically altered with DFs over a portion of edges in visual film, including various individuals' countenances. The parallel order strategy should be moved up to multi-class/multi-mark and neighborhood characterization/discovery at the casing level to manage the difficulties of accurate settings.

### 4.6.3 STRATEGIES FOR IDENTIFICATION HAVE AN ABSENCE OF REASONABLENESS

Existing DF recognition strategies commonly work to dissect a significant dataset in groups. Be that as it may, when writers or law requirements utilize these instruments in the field, there may just be few accounts accessible for examination. Suppose a mathematical score relating to the probability of a genuine or counterfeit sound or video can't be checked with legitimate evidence of the score. In that case, it isn't as significant to experts. In specific cases, it's ordinary to look for clarification for the mathematical score altogether for the examination to be accepted before it's distributed or utilized in court. Be that as it may, most DFs location calculations, primarily those dependent on DL draws near, need such clarification because of their discovery nature.

### 4.6.4 TRANSIENT AGGREGATION

DF location moves toward now being used depending on paired grouping at the casing level; for example, deciding the probability of every video outline being genuine or controlled. These methodologies, then again, don't consider fleeting consistency between methods, which can prompt two issues:

i)   DF content can show fleeting antiquities, and
ii)  genuine or counterfeit edges can happen in consecutive spans.

Besides, these strategies require a different stage to process the video trustworthiness score, as they should coordinate the scores from each casing to show up at an end-product.

### 4.6.5 LAUNDERING ON SOCIAL MEDIA

The primary web networks used to spread general media data among general society are social stages such as Twitter, Facebook, and Instagram. Before transferring, such substance is deprived of meta-information, down-examined, and seriously compacted to moderate network transmission capacity or ensure the client's protection. These modifications, otherwise called online media laundering, eliminate the signs of basic phonies and, thus, increment the quantity of bogus upsides distinguished. Online media laundering significantly affects most DF recognition strategies that utilize signal-level central issues. The consideration of recreations of these impacts in preparing information, just as extending the evaluation datasets to remember information for web-based media washed visual material, is one way of working on the precision of DF ID calculations over online media laundering.

## 4.7 SUMMARY

Face trading recordings are the most widely recognized objective of late DF recognition methods, and most of the transferred counterfeit recordings fall into this class.

   i.   identification of antiques leftover from the age interaction; for example, irregularities in the head present [59], absence of eye squinting [60], shading varieties in facial surface [61], and teeth arrangement,
  ii.   detection of inconspicuous GAN-produced tests,
 iii.   spatial transient provisions, and
  iv.   psychological signals such as pulse [62] and a singular's conduct standards [63].

Notwithstanding how much work has been done in robotized identification, there is still space for improvement.

*   Existing approaches are defenseless against post-handling cycles such as pressure, commotion impacts, and light changes, among others. Furthermore, just a limited quantity of exploration has been given to identifying sound and visual DFs.
*   Most late systems have focused on face-trade recognition by utilizing blemishes like visual antiques. Notwithstanding, as innovation propels, more modern face trades, for example, impersonating somebody with a comparative face shape, character, and hairstyle, will become conceivable sooner rather than later. Different kinds of DF, such as face-reenactment and lip-synchronizing, are becoming more famous.
*   By expanding reproduced signal-level central issues utilized by existing recognizable proof strategies, hostile to legal methodologies can name a unique video as a DF, a state, we call counterfeit DF.
*   Furthermore, to battle DFs, a few essayists proposed utilizing the blockchain and smart contracts ideas to perceive legal modifications done inside visual substance [64,65]. Indeed, even within the sight of other control assaults, Sutton [65] utilized Ethereum keen agreements to find and track the beginning and history of adjusted data and its source. This intelligent contract used the interplanetary record framework's hashes to save recordings alongside their metadata. This technique might be viable for recognizing DFs, but it is helpful if video metadata is accessible. Utilizing negligible datasets to identify DFs using AI material science: DF finders endure troubles attributable to fragmented, meager, and loud information in the preparation cycle. Imaginative AI structures, calculations, and approaches that "prepare in" material science,

arithmetic, and earlier report pertinent to DFs should have been investigated. Utilizing information injected figuring out how to install material science and earlier statement into AI will help beat the difficulties of inadequate information and work with the structure of causal and logical generative models.

- Existing DF identifiers have fundamentally depended on fixed parts of existing digital assaults through AI procedures; for example, unaided bunching and managed grouping draws near, making them less inclined to recognize obscure DFs. Subsequently, reinforcement learning (RL) [66] strategies might assume a critical part in the distinguishing proof of DFs later on.
- Because many muddled DFs comprise transient successions of dynamic practices, strategies like [67] could be used to plan a discovery challenge to a Markov-chain state esteem forecast task. The state esteem expectation model may be the direct transient contrast (TD) RL calculation [67], with the outcomes contrasted with a predetermined edge to recognize authentic and DF curios. Then again, you may use the bit-based RL procedure with least-squares TD. The TD RL's speculation ability is improved by applying piece draws near, remarkably in high-dimensional and nonlinear element fields. Subsequently, the part least squares TD procedure may be utilized to dependably assess peculiarity probabilities, hence expanding the viability of a DF identifier.
- The expected provisions (for example, different visual and sound phonies, and so forth) needed to assess the viability of more vigorous DF discovery calculations are missing from existing DFs datasets. Established researchers have ignored how DF films contain visual fabrications and sound adjustment. DF datasets are accessible survey visual forgeries and overlook sound fabrications. Cloning and voice replay ridiculing may have a more significant impact in DF video age soon. In DF recordings, shallow sound imitations can be joined with deep sound phonies. We have made a discourse mocking recognition corpus [67]. We are presently dealing with creating a solid voice cloning and general media DF dataset that can be utilized to test the adequacy of cutting-edge available media DF identification frameworks.

The next chapter will focus on development of image translating model to counter adversarial attacks.

## REFERENCES

[1] M. Westerlund, "The emergence of DF technology: A review," Technology Innovation Management Review, vol. 9, no. 11, pp. 39–52, 2019.

[2] D. Güera and E. J. Delp, "DF video detection using recurrent neural networks," in 2018 15th IEEE International Conference on Advanced Video and Signal Based Surveillance (AVSS), pp. 1–6, 2018.

[3] K. Saxena and N. John, "DF is a fast-growing monster. Here's why man and machine must join hands to tame it," The Economic Times, 2019 [Online]. Available at: https://prime.economictimes.indiatimes.com/news/69050623/technology-and-startups/DF-is-a-fast-growing-monster-heres-why-man-and-machine-must-join-hands-to-tame-it-

[4] D. Harris, "DFs: False pornography is here and the law cannot protect you," Duke L. Tech. Rev., vol. 17, pp. 99–127, 2018.

[5] J. Fletcher, "AI, and some kind of dystopia: The new faces of online post-fact performance," Theatre Journal, vol. 70, no. 4, pp. 455–471, 2018.

[6] C. Vaccari and A. Chadwick, "DFs and disinformation: Exploring the impact of synthetic political video on deception, uncertainty, and trust in news," Social Media+ Society, vol. 6, no. 1, pp. 1–13, 2020.

[7] M. Albahar and J. Almalki, "DFs: Threats and countermeasures systematic review," Journal of Theoretical and Applied Information Technology, vol. 97, no. 22, pp. 3242–3250, 2019.

[8] S. Catherine, "Fraudsters used AI to mimic CEO's voice in unusual cybercrime case," The Wall Street Journal, 2019 [Online]. Available at: www.wsj.com/articles/fraudst ers-use-ai-to-mimic-ceos-voice-in-unusual-cybercrime-case-11567157402?mod= searchresults&page=1&pos=1

[9] S. Raphael, "Experts: Spy used AI-generated face to connect with targets," AP NEWS, 2019 [Online]. Available at: https://apnews.com/bc2f19097a4c4fffaa00de6770b8a60d

[10] X. Yang, Y. Li, and S. Lyu, "Exposing deep fakes using inconsistent head poses," ICASSP 2019–2019 IEEE International Conference on Acoustics, Speech and Signal Processing (ICASSP), pp. 8261–8265, 2019.

[11] P. Korshunov and S. Marcel, "DFs: A new threat to face recognition? Assessment and detection," arXiv preprint arXiv:1812.08685, 2018.

[12] "Vidtimit," [Online]. Available at: http://conradsanderson.id.au/vidtimit/

[13] A. Rossler, D. Cozzolino, L. Verdoliva, C. Riess, J. Thies, and M. Nießner, "Faceforensics++: Learning to detect manipulated facial images," in Proceedings of the IEEE International Conference on Computer Vision, pp. 1–11, 2019.

[14] "DFdetection," [Online]. Available at: https://ai.googleblog.com/2019/09/contribut ing-data-to-DFs-detection.html

[15] "DFs detection challenge," [Online]. Available at: https://DFdetectionchallenge.ai

[16] Y. Z. Li, X. Yang, P. Sun, H. G. Qi, and S. W. Lyu, "Celeb-df: A large-scale challenging dataset for DFs forensics," arXiv preprint arXiv:1909.12962, 2019.

[17] "Celeb-df(v2)," [Online]. Available at: www.cs.albany.edu/~lsw/celebDFforens ics.html

[18] S. Lorant, Lincoln; a picture story of his life. Norton, 1969 [Online]. Available at: www. amazon.com/dp/0393074463

[19] J. Thies, M. Zollh¨ofer, M. Stamminger, C. Theobalt, and M. Nießner, "Face2Face:Real-time face capture and reenactment of RGB videos," Proceedings of the IEEE Conference on Computer Vision and Pattern Recognition, pp. 2387–2395, Jun. 2016, Las Vegas, NV [Online]. Available at: https://doi.org/10.1109/CVPR.2016.262

[20] D. K. Sharma, L. Gaur, and D. Okunbor, "Image compression and feature extraction with neural network," Proceedings of the Academy of Information and Management Sciences, 11(1), pp. 33–38, 2007.

[21] J. Y. Zhu, T. Park, P. Isola, and A. A. Efros, "Unpaired image-to-image translation using cycle-consistent adversarial networks," Proceedings of the IEEE International Conference on Computer Vision, pp. 2242–2251, Oct. 2017, Venice, Italy [Online]. Available at: https://doi.org/10.1109/ICCV.2017.244

[22] M. Abadi, P. Barham, J. Chen, Z. Chen, A. Davis, J. Dean, M. Devin, S. Ghemawat, G. Irving, M. Isard, et al., "Tensorflow: A system for large-scale ML." Proceedings of the USENIX Conference on Operating Systems Design and Implementation, vol. 16, pp. 265–283, Nov. 2016, Savannah, GA [Online]. Available at: www.usenix.org/confere nce/osdi16/technicalsessions/presentation/abadi

[23] F. Chollet, et al., "Keras," https://keras.io, 2015.

[24] A. Tewari, M. Zollh¨ofer, H. Kim, P. Garrido, F. Bernard, P. P´erez, and C. Theobalt, "MoFA: Model-based deep convolutional face autoencoder for unsupervised monocular reconstruction," Proceedings of the IEEE International Conference on Computer Vision, pp. 3735–3744, Oct. 2017, Venice, Italy [Online]. Available at: https://doi.org/10.1109/ICCV.2017.401

[25] I. Goodfellow, J. Pouget-Abadie, M. Mirza, B. Xu, D. Warde-Farley, S. Ozair, A. Courville, and Y. Bengio, "Generative adversarial nets," Advances in Neural Information Processing Systems, pp. 2672–2680, Dec. 2014, Montréal, Canada [Online]. Available at: http://papers.nips.cc/paper/5423-generative-adversarial-nets

[26] G. Antipov, M. Baccouche, and J.-L. Dugelay, "Face aging with conditional GANs," arXiv:1702.01983v2, Feb. 2017 [Online]. Available at: https://arxiv.org/abs/1702.01983v2

[27] K. Dale, K. Sunkavalli, M. K. Johnson, D. Vlasic, W. Matusik, and H. Pfister, "Video face replacement," ACM Transactions on Graphics, vol. 30, no. 6, pp. 1–130, Dec. 2011 [Online]. Available at: https://doi.org/10.1145/2070781.2024164

[28] "Fakeapp," www.fakeapp.org/

[29] C. Bregler, M. Covell, and M. Slaney, "Video rewrite: Driving visual speech with audio," Proceedings of the ACM Annual Conference on Computer Graphics and Interactive Techniques, pp. 353–360, Aug. 1997, Los Angeles, CA [Online]. Available at: https://doi.org/10.1145/258734.258880

[30] H. Averbuch-Elor, D. Cohen-Or, J. Kopf, and M. F. Cohen, "Bringing portraits to life," ACM Transactions on Graphics, vol. 36, no. 6, pp. 196:1–196:13, Nov. 2017 [Online]. Available at: https://doi.org/10.1145/3130800.3130818

[31] Z. Lu, Z. Li, J. Cao, R. He, and Z. Sun, "Recent progress of face image synthesis," arXiv:1706.04717v1, Jun. 2017 [Online]. Available at: https://arxiv.org/abs/1706.04717v1

[32] Y. Lu, Y.-W. Tai, and C.-K. Tang, "Attribute-guided face generation using conditional CycleGAN," Proceedings of the European Conference on Computer Vision, pp. 293–308, Oct. 2018, Munich, Germany [Online]. Available at: https://doi.org/10.1007/978-3-030-01258-8n18

[33] P. Upchurch, J. Gardner, G. Pleiss, R. Pless, N. Snavely, K. Bala, and K. Weinberger, "Deep feature interpolation for image content changes," Proceedings of the IEEE Conference on Computer Vision and Pattern Recognition, pp. 6090–6099, Jul. 2017, Honolulu, HI [Online]. Available at: https://doi.org/10.1109/CVPR.2017.645

[34] G. Lample, G. Lample, N. Zeghidour, N. Usunier, A. Bordes, L. Denoyer, and M. Ranzato, "Fader networks: Manipulating images by sliding attributes," Advances in Neural Information Processing Systems, pp. 5967–5976, Dec. 2017, Long Beach, CA [Online]. Available at: https://papers.nips.cc/paper/7178-fadernetworksmanipulating-images-by-sliding-attributes

[35] T. Karras, T. Aila, S. Laine, and J. Lehtinen, "Progressive growing of GANs for improved quality, stability, and variation," Proceedings of the International Conference on Learning Representations, Apr. 2018 [Online]. Available at: https://openreview.net/forum?id=Hk99zCeAb

[36] S. Hochreiter and J. Schmidhuber, "Long short-term memory," Neural Computation, vol. 9, no. 8, pp. 1735–1780, Nov. 1997 [Online]. Available at: https://doi.org/10.1162/neco.1997.9.8.1735

[37] D. Güera and E. J. Delp, "DF video detection using recurrent neural networks," 2018 15th IEEE International Conference on Advanced Video and Signal Based Surveillance (AVSS), pp. 1–6, 2018.

[38] K. Simonyan and A. Zisserman, "Very deep convolutional networks for largescale image recognition," arXiv preprint arXiv:1409.1556, 2014.

[39] C. Szegedy, V. Vanhoucke, S. Ioffe, J. Shlens, and Z. Wojna, "Rethinking the inception architecture for computer vision," Proceedings of the IEEE Conference on Computer Vision and Pattern Recognition, pp. 2818–2826, 2016.

[40] J. Donahue, L. A. Hendricks, S. Guadarrama, M. Rohrbach, S. Venugopalan, K. Saenko, and T. Darrell, "Long-term recurrent convolutional networks for visual recognition and description," in CVPR, pp. 2625–2634, 2015.

[41] Y. Li, M. C. Chang, and S. Lyu, "In ictu oculi: Exposing AI created fake videos by detecting eye blinking," 2018 IEEE International Workshop on Information Forensics and Security (WIFS), pp. 1–7, 2018.

[42] D. Afchar, V. Nozick, J. Yamagishi, and I. Echizen, "Mesonet: A compact facial video forgery detection network," 2018 IEEE International Workshop on Information Forensics and Security (WIFS), pp. 1–7, 2018.

[43] S. Ioffe and C. Szegedy, "Batch normalization: Accelerating deep network training by reducing internal covariate shift," arXiv preprint arXiv:1502.03167, pp. 1–7, 2015.

[44] N. Murray and F. Perronnin, "Generalized max pooling," in Proceedings of the IEEE Conference on Computer Vision and Pattern Recognition, pp. 2473–2480, 2014.

[45] Y. Li and S. Lyu, "Exposing DF videos by detecting face warping artifacts," arXiv preprint arXiv:1811.00656, 2018.

[46] K. He, X. Y. Zhang, S. Q. Ren, and J. Sun, "Deep residual learning for image recognition," in Proceedings of the IEEE conference on computer vision and pattern recognition, pp. 770–778, 2016.

[47] C. C. Chang and C. J. Lin, "Libsvm: A library for support vector machines," ACM transactions on intelligent systems and technology (TIST), vol. 2, no. 3, pp. 1–27, 2011.

[48] J. Wu, K. Feng, X. Chang, X, and T. Yang, "A forensic method for DF image based on face recognition," in Proceedings of the 2020 4th High Performance Computing and Cluster Technologies Conference 2020 3rd International Conference on Big Data and AI, pp. 104–108, 2020.

[49] X. Yang, Y. Li, and S. Lyu, "Exposing deep fakes using inconsistent head poses," ICASSP 2019–2019 IEEE International Conference on Acoustics, Speech and Signal Processing (ICASSP), pp. 8261–8265, 2019.

[50] F. Matern, C. Riess, and M. Stamminger, "Exploiting visual artifacts to expose DFs and face manipulations," 2019 IEEE Winter Applications of Computer Vision Workshops (WACVW), pp. 83–92, 2019.

[51] C. Chen, M. N. Do, and J. Wang, "Robust image and video dehazing with visual artifact suppression via gradient residual minimization," in European Conference on Computer Vision, pp. 576–591, 2016.

[52] J. Thies, M. Zollhofe, M. Stamminger, C. Theobalt, and M. Nießner, "Face2face: Realtime face capture and reenactment of rgb videos," Proceedings of the IEEE Conference on Computer Vision and Pattern Recognition, pp. 2387–2395, 2016.

[53] G. Singh, B. Kumar, L. Gaur and A. Tyagi (2019), "Comparison between Multinomial and Bernoulli Naïve Bayes for Text Classification," *2019 International Conference on Automation, Computational and Technology Management (ICACTM)*, pp. 593–596. doi:10.1109/ICACTM.2019.8776800.

[54] T. Windeatt, "Ensemble mlp classifier design," in Computational Intelligence Paradigms, pp. 133–147, 2008.

[55] M. A. Mansournia, A. Geroldinger, S. Greenland, and G. Heinze, "Separation in logistic regression: Causes, consequences, and control," American Journal of Epidemiology, vol. 187, no. 4, pp. 864–870, 2018.

[56] L. Gaur, U. Bhatia, N. Z. Jhanjhi, G. Muhammad, and M. Masud (2021). Medical image-based detection of COVID-19 using deep convolution neural networks. Multimedia Systems. doi:10.1007/s00530-021-00794-6

[57] T. Soukupova and J. Cech, "Eye blink detection using facial landmarks," in 21st Computer Vision Winter Workshop, Rimske Toplice, Slovenia, 2016.

[58] S. McCloskey and M. Albright, "Detecting GAN-generated imagery using color cues," arXiv preprint arXiv:.08247, 2018.

[59] S. Fernandes, et al., "Predicting heart rate variations of DF videos using neural ODE," in Proceedings of the IEEE International Conference on Computer Vision Workshops, 2019.

[60] S. Agarwal, H. Farid, Y. Gu, M. He, K. Nagano, and H. Li, "Protecting world leaders against Deep Fakes," in Proceedings of the IEEE Conference on Computer Vision and Pattern Recognition Workshops, pp. 38–45, 2019.

[61] P. Fraga-Lamas and T. M. Fernández-Caramés, "Fake news, disinformation, and DFs: Leveraging distributed ledger technologies and blockchain to combat digital deception and counterfeit reality," IT Professional, vol. 22, no. 2, pp. 53–59, 2020.

[62] H. R. Hasan and K. Salah, "Combating DF videos using blockchain and smart contracts," IEEE Access, vol. 7, pp. 41596–41606, 2019.

[63] M. Feng and H. Xu, "Deep reinforecement learning based optimal defense for cyber-physical system in presence of unknown cyber-attack," in 2017 IEEE Symposium Series on Computational Intelligence (SSCI), pp. 1–8, 2017: IEEE.

[64] X. Xu and T. Xie, "A reinforcement learning approach for host-based intrusion detection using sequences of system calls," in International Conference on Intelligent Computing, pp. 995–1003, 2005: Springer.

[65] R. S. Sutton, "Learning to predict by the methods of temporal differences," ML, vol. 3, no. 1, pp. 9–44, 1988.

[66] Gaur, L., Singh, G., Solanki, A., Jhanjhi, N. Z., Bhatia, U., Sharma, S., … and Kim, W. (2021), "Disposition of youth in predicting sustainable development goals using the neuro-fuzzy and random forest algorithms" Human-Centric Computing and Information Sciences, 11, NA.

[67] R. Baumann, K. M. Malik, A. Javed, A. Ball, B. Kujawa, and H. Malik, "Voice spoofing detection corpus for single and multi-order audio replays," Computer Speech Language, vol. 65, p. 101132, 2021.

# 5 Development of Image Translating Model to Counter Adversarial Attacks

*Loveleen Gaur, Mohan Bhandari, and*
*Tanvi Razdan*

## CONTENTS

## 5.1 INTRODUCTION

DeepFakes (DFs), or facially modified photos and videos, can be used offensively to spread misinformation or discredit someone. DFs use AI to superimpose voices and likenesses, allowing them to put someone else's words in their mouth essentially. DFs proliferate throughout mainstream and social media, and these sources are scrambling to control the spread of potentially misleading information on their platforms [1]. As a result, recognizing DFs is critical for improving the trustworthiness of social media platforms and other media-sharing websites. DF detection approaches that are now in use rely on neural-network-based classification models that have been revealed to be weak to adversarial examples [2].

    DL is at the core of AI's present ascent. It has become the backbone of the field of computer vision [3]. With the recent advancements in the field of computer vision [4,5] and natural language processing [6], together, they are putting trained classifiers in the center of mission-critical security systems. Applications ranging from self-driving automobiles to surveillance and security are all prime examples. As a result of these developments, ML security is becoming increasingly vital. Resistance to adversarially chosen inputs, in particular, is becoming a critical design aim. While trained models are usually quite good at categorizing innocuous inputs, new research shows that they aren't always the same. Several works [7,8,9] demonstrate how an adversary can frequently alter input to cause the model to provide an inaccurate output. Small alterations to the input image can trick the state-of-the-art neural networks with high confidence, making computer vision an especially compelling challenge [10].

Ultramodern and advanced deep neural networks (DNNs) are highly effective in solving many complex real-world problems but are subject to adversarial examples, posing a security risk to these algorithms because of the possibly severe outcomes. Before DL models are implemented, adversarial attacks are used as a proxy to test their resilience. On the other hand, most adversarial attacks can only deceive a black-box model with a low success rate [11]. It remains true even though the benign case was accurately categorized, and the alteration is undetectable to humans. Aside from the security considerations, this evidence explains that our existing models aren't consistently learning the fundamental ideas. Adversarial attacks are algorithms that find highly resembled images to cheat a classifier. Training classifiers under adversarial attack has become one of the most profitable ways to enhance the sturdiness of classifiers [12]. General Adversarial Network (GAN) is a generative model where the generator learns to convert white noise to images that look authentic to the discriminator [13,14].

The phenomena of adversarial examples—intentionally generated inputs that deceive trained ML models—have piqued the academic community's interest in recent years, mainly when limited to minor changes to a correctly interpreted input. It is also seen that image classifiers also underachieve on randomly distorted images, such as images with additive Gaussian noise [15]. Many sophisticated techniques based on the *Lp* distance for penalizing perturbations have been developed to produce adversarial examples. To protect against such adversarial attacks, researchers have looked at various defense mechanisms. The use of *Lp* distance as a gauge of perceptual quality is still under investigation [16].

Due to their complexity, it is challenging to identify how ML models might misbehave or be abused when deployed. Recent work on adversarial instances, or inputs with modest alterations that result in significantly different model predictions, has helped assess the robustness of these models by highlighting the hostile circumstances where they fail. On the other hand, these intentional disturbances are frequently artificial, lack semantic meaning, and are inapplicable to complex domains like language [17].

## 5.2 RELATED WORK

Ruiz et al. [18] proposed and successfully applied class transferable adversarial attacks that generalize to different classes and adversarial training for GANs as the first step toward robust image translation networks. They devised a spread-spectrum adversarial attack capable of eluding blur defenses. Their method achieves better performance on the Gaussian blur scenarios with a high blur magnitude. Their solution outperforms the competition in Gaussian blur cases with large blur magnitudes. Their iterative spread-spectrum technique is roughly K times faster than expectation over transformation (EoT) since each iteration of Iterative Fast Gradient Sign Method (I-FGSM) requires only one forward–backward pass instead of K to compute the loss.

Qiu et al. [19] comprehensively summarize the latest research progress on adversarial attack and defense technologies in deep learning. The findings suggested that when compared with the black-box attacks, the white-box attacks have higher success rates, enabling the target model to achieve an error rate of approximately 89%–99%. Although the attack success rates of black-box attacks, which lead to an error rate of roughly 84%–96%, are not as reasonable as that of white-box attacks, since black-box attacks do not need to know any information of the target model, the adversarial attacks can be carried out by utilizing the transferability of adversarial samples, model inversion, and model extraction.

Finlayson et al. [20] proposed and deployed models representing the current state of the art in medical computer vision. All the baseline models achieved performance reasonably consistent with the results reported in the original manuscripts on natural images: AUROC of 0.910 for diabetic retinopathy, AUROC of 0.936 for pneumothorax, and AUROC of 0.86 on melanoma. Projected gradient descent attacks, targeting the incorrect answer in every case, produced effective AUROCs of 0.000 and accuracies of 0% for all white-box attacks. Black-box attacks produced AUROCs of less than 0.10 for all tasks, and accuracies ranged from 0.01% on fundoscopy to 37.9% on dermoscopy. Qualitatively, all attacks were human-imperceptible. Adversarial patch attacks also achieved effective AUROCs of 0.000 and accuracies of <1% for white-box attacks on all tasks. Black-box adversarial patch attacks reached AUROCs of less than 0.005 for all tasks and accuracies less than 10%. The "natural patch" controls created by adding patches created from the most strongly classified image of the desired class resulted in AUROCs ranging from 0.48 to 0.83 with accuracies ranging from 67.5% to 92.1%.

Samangouei et al. [21] proposed Defense-GAN, a new framework leveraging the expressive capability of generative models to defend DNNs against such attacks. It is trained to model the distribution of unperturbed images. It finds a close output to a given image that does not contain the adversarial changes. This output is then fed to the classifier. The proposed method can be used with any classification model and does not modify the classifier structure or training procedure. The performance of Defense-GAN-Rec and that of Defense-GAN-Orig are very close, and MagNet achieves lower accuracy than Defense-GAN.

Santhanam and Grnarova [22] proposed cowboy, an approach to detecting and defending against adversarial attacks by using the discriminator and generator of a GAN trained on the same dataset. The discriminator consistently scores the adversarial samples lower than the real samples across multiple attacks and datasets in this approach. They also put forward a cleaning method that uses both the discriminator and generator of the GAN to project the samples back onto the data manifold. This cleaning procedure is independent of the classifier and attack type and can thus be deployed in existing systems.

Hu and Tan [23] offer MalGAN, a GAN-based approach for generating adversarial malware instances that can circumvent black-box ML-based detection models. To fit the black-box malware detection system, MalGAN employs a substitute detector. A generative network is trained to reduce the malicious probabilities predicted by the substitution detector in the generated adversarial samples. MalGAN outperforms typical gradient-based adversarial example generation techniques by lowering the detection rate to practically zero and making retraining-based defensive methods against adversarial examples challenging to implement. According to the experimental data, the created adversarial examples can effectively evade the black-box detector. Malware makers can immediately crack the black-box detector once it has been updated.

Gandhi and Jain [24] created adversarial perturbations using the Fast Gradient Sign Method (FGSM) and the Carlini and Wagner L2 norm to produce adversarial perturbations. On unperturbed DFs, detectors obtained more than 95% accuracy but less than 27% accuracy on perturbed DFs. They discovered that the Digital Image Processing (DIP) defense eliminates disturbances unsupervised using generative convolutional neural networks. On average, regularization increased the detection of perturbed DFs, with a 10% improvement in the black-box scenario. On a 100 picture subsample, the DIP defense achieved 95% accuracy on perturbed DFs that deceived the original detector while maintaining 98% accuracy in other circumstances.

Liu and Hsieh [25] create the Rob-GAN framework to collectively optimize the generator and discriminator in the face of adversarial attacks—the generator generates fake images to trick the discriminator. In contrast, the adversarial attacker perturbs authentic photos to fool the discriminator, and the discriminator wants to minimize loss under both fake and adversarial images. According to the findings, the generated classifier is more resilient than the state-of-the-art adversarial training strategy, and the generator beats SN-GAN on ImageNet-143.

Croce and Hein [26] suggest a black-box method for creating adversarial samples to reduce the 10-distance from the source picture. Extensive testing has revealed that the attack is superior to or competitive with the current state of the art. Furthermore, it can incorporate additional component-wise perturbation constraints. The adversarial examples are practically undetectable because the authors only allowed pixels to change in high-variation zones and avoid changes along axis-aligned edges. The Projected Gradient Descent attack was also modified to account for the 10-norm integrating component-wise limitation, enabling the model to do adversarial training to improve classifier resilience against sparse and imperceptible adversarial alterations.

Zhang and Wang [27] present a feature scattering-based adversarial training method for increasing model resilience against adversarial attacks. The suggested method uses feature dispersion in the latent space to produce adversarial images for training, which is unsupervised and eliminates label leakage. More crucially, this novel method makes altered pictures collaboratively, considering inter-sample interactions.

Liao et al. [28] offer high-level representation guided denoiser (HGD) as a defense for image categorization. Using a loss function defined as the difference between the target model's outputs activated by the clean picture and denoised image, HGD avoids the error amplification phenomenon, in which modest residual adversarial noise is progressively amplified and leads to incorrect classification. HGD provides several benefits over adversarial ensemble training, the current state-of-the-art defense approach on huge pictures.

Mustafa et al. [29] introduce a computationally efficient picture-enhancing method with a robust defense mechanism to limit the influence of adversarial perturbations successfully. They show that deep image restoration networks can learn mapping functions that move adversarial samples from off-the-manifold onto the natural picture manifold, restoring classification to proper classes. The technique is unique in that it improves picture quality while still maintaining model performance on clean images and offering resilience against assaults. Furthermore, the suggested solution does not require a separate system to detect adversarial pictures and does not require any modifications to the classifier. Extensive trials have shown the scheme's efficiency in gray-box scenarios.

Song et al. [30] suggested using the lossy Saak transform as a preprocessing tool to protect against adversarial attacks on adversarially perturbed images. They found that the Saak transform's outputs are highly good at distinguishing between adversarial and clean samples [31,32,33]. The picture after processing is shown to be resistant to adversarial perturbations. On both the CIFAR10 and ImageNet datasets, their model beats the state-of-the-art adversarial defensive strategies by a significant margin without compromising judgment performance on clean pictures. Importantly, our findings imply that adversarial perturbations [34,35,36] may be effectively and efficiently resisted by employing the state-of-the-art frequency analysis.

## 5.3 DATASETS

In this study, we used a publicly available MNIST dataset. The MNIST database contains 60,000 training images and 10,000 testing images. Half of the training set and half of the test set were taken from NIST's training dataset, while the other half of the training set and the other half of the test set were taken from NIST's testing dataset.

## 5.4 DATA PRE-PROCESSING

MNIST images are 28 × 28 pixels, but they are zero-padded to 32 × 32 pixels and normalized before being fed to the network. The rest of the network does not use any padding, so the size keeps shrinking as the image progresses through the web.

## 5.5 METHODOLOGY

FGSM involves adding noise (not random noise) that has the same direction as the cost function's gradient concerning the data. The noise is adjusted by epsilon, usually bound by the max norm to be a small integer. An adversarial example is a portion of the input data that has been slightly altered to induce the algorithm to misclassify it.

In our experiment, we have the input as the original image F(X) and output as the Adversarial Image F(X') in between is the neural network process in which the algorithm, at first, collects the element-wise sign of the data gradient from F(X) and then creates the perturbed image F(X') by adjusting each pixel of the input image after which it adds clipping to maintain [0,1] range; this goes on until the algorithm "correctly" misclassifies the image and only then it returns to the troubled image.

If it fails to misclassify the image, the same steps are followed again by the algorithm, and the neural network adjusts the [37,38,39] weights each time until the algorithm can finally produce the adversarial image.

Suppose we talk about the neural network's role, a hidden layer between the algorithm's input and output, which applies weights to the inputs and guides them via an activation function as the output. The hidden layers alter the inputs into the network in a nonlinear fashion. The purpose of the neural network determines the hidden layers, and the layers themselves may change based on their associated weights. Hidden layers are a series of mathematical functions, each of which gives an output that is particular to the desired outcome. Squashing functions, for example, are certain types of hidden layers. Because they accept input and create an output value between 0 and 1, the range for defining probability, these functions are beneficial when the algorithm's desired result is a probability. Hidden layers allow a neural network's function to be split into particular data modifications. Each function in the hidden layer is tailored to generate an inevitable result (see Figure 5.1).

The overall breakdown of the process includes the following:

1. Calculate the loss after forwarding propagation,
2. Calculate the gradient concerning the pixels of the image,
3. Nudge the image pixels ever so slightly in the direction of the calculated gradients that maximize the loss calculated above.

While calculating the loss after forwarding propagation, we use a negative likelihood loss function to estimate how close the prediction of our model is to the actual class. Calculating gradients, we determine [40,41,42] the direction in which to nudge your weights to reduce the loss value. We adjust the input image pixels in the direction of the gradients to maximize the loss value.

When training neural networks, the most popular way of determining the direction to adjust a particular weight deep in the network (that is, the gradient of the loss function concerning that particular weight) is by back-propagating the gradients from the start (output part) to the weight. We back-propagate the gradients from the output layer to the input image [43,44,45]. In ML, to nudge the weights to decrease the loss value, we use this simple equation:

*new_weights = old_weights − learning_rate * gradients*

We apply the same concept for FGSM, but we want to maximize the loss, so we nudge the pixel values of the image according to the following equation:

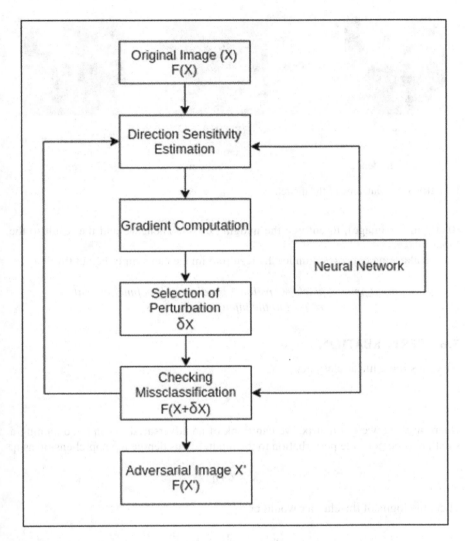

**FIGURE 5.1** Flowchart.

$$new\_pixels = old\_pixels + epsilon * gradients$$

X represents the input image that we want the model to predict wrongly in the above image (see Figure 5.2).

The second part of the image represents the gradients of the loss function concerning the input image.

Remember that the gradient is just a directional tensor (it gives information about which direction to move in). We multiply the gradients with a very tiny value, epsilon

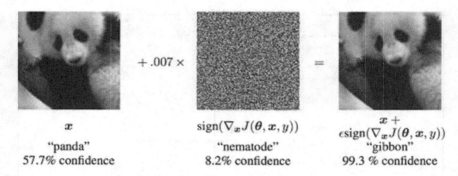

FIGURE 5.2　Outcome of the model.

(0.007 in the image), to enforce the nudging effect. Then, we add the result to the input image.

The alarming expression under the resulting image can simply be put this way:

*input_image_pixels + epsilon \* gradient of loss function with respect to the input_image_pixels*

## 5.6　PERTURBATION

Given a simple linear classifier

$$w^\mathsf{T}x$$

where $w$ is the weight matrix, we can think of an adversarial example containing a small, non-perceivable perturbation to the input. Let us denote the apprehension as $\eta$.

$$x' = x + \eta$$

Then, the logits of the classier would be

$$w^\mathsf{T}x' = w^\mathsf{T}(x + \eta)$$

$$= w^\mathsf{T}x + w^\mathsf{T}\eta$$

It means that, given a small perturbation $\eta$, the perturbation's actual effect on the classifier's logits is given by $w^\mathsf{T}\eta$. The underlying idea behind FGSM is that we can find some $\eta$ that causes a change that is non-perceivable and ostensibly innocuous to the human eye, yet destructive and adverse enough for the classifier to the extent that its predictions are no longer accurate.

Let us put this into context by considering an example. Say we have some image classifier that receives RBG images as input. Typical RGB images have integer pixel values ranging from 0 to 255. These values are typically preprocessed through division by 255. Hence, the precision of data is limited by this eight-bit bottleneck. It means that, for perturbations below 1/255, we should not expect the classifier to output a different prediction. In other words, the addition of $w^T\eta$ should not cause the model to behave any additional in the absence of any perturbation.

An adversarial example maximizes the value of $w^T\eta$ to sway the model into making a wrong prediction. Of course, there is a constraint on $\eta$; otherwise, we could just apply a huge perturbation to the input image, but then the perturbation could be visible enough to change the ground truth label. Hence, we apply a constraint such that

$$\|\eta\|\infty \leq \epsilon \|\eta\|\infty \leq \epsilon$$

The infinity norm is defined as

$$\|A\|\infty = \max \ (1 \leq i \leq m) \Sigma j = 1 n |aij|$$

more simply put, which means the largest absolute value of the element in the matrix or vector. In this context, it means that the largest magnitude of the element in $\eta$ does not exceed the precision constraint $\epsilon$.

Then, Goodfellow proceeds to explain the maximum bounds of this perturbation. Namely, given that

$$\eta = \epsilon \cdot sign(w)$$

the maximum bound of the change inactivation can be written as

$$w^T\eta = \epsilon \cdot w^T \ sign(w)$$

$$= \epsilon \|w\| 1$$

$$= \epsilon mn$$

where the average magnitude of an element of w is given by m, and $w \in Rn$.

It tells us that the change in activation provided by the perturbation increases linearly concerning n or the dimension. In other words, in sufficiently high-dimensional contexts, we can expect even a small perturbation capped at $\epsilon$ to produce a perturbation significant enough to render the model susceptible to an adversarial attack. Such perturbed examples are referred to as adversarial examples.

## 5.7 GRADIENT

The above equations demonstrated that the degree of perturbation increases as dimensionality increases. In other words, we established that creating adversarial examples is possible via infinitesimal perturbations. In this section, let us dive into the specifics of FGSM.

The idea behind FGSM is surprisingly simple: we do the opposite of the typical gradient descent to maximize the loss since confusing the model is the end goal of an adversarial attack. Therefore, we consider xx, the model's input, a trainable parameter. Then, we add the gradient to its original input variable to create a perturbation. Mathematically, this can be expressed as follows:

$$\eta = \epsilon \cdot \text{sign}(\nabla x J(w,x,y))$$

where JJ represents the cost function. Then, we can create an adversarial example via

$$x' = x + \epsilon \cdot \text{sign}(\nabla x J(w,x,y))$$

It is the crux of the FGSM: we use the gradient sign, multiply it by some small value, and add that perturbation to the original input to create an adversarial example.

One way to look at this is in terms of first-order approximation. Recall that

$$f(x') \simeq f(x) + (x'-x)^T \nabla x f(x)$$

In this context, we can consider ff to be the cost function JJ, which then turns into

$$J(w,x') = J(x,w) + (x'-x)^T \nabla x J(w,x)$$

Then, the goal of an adversarial attack is to maximize the second term in addition. Since there is an infinity norm constraint on the perturbation, namely

$$\|x'-x\|\infty \leq \epsilon$$

with some thinking, we can convince ourselves that the perturbed example that maximizes the loss function is given by

$$x' = x + \epsilon \cdot \text{sign}(\nabla x J(w,x,y))$$

## 5.8   RESULT AND DISCUSSION

### 5.8.1   ATTACK SETTINGS

We focus on the difficulty of an adversarial attack on MNIST images. The attack difficulty is measured by the least maximum perturbation required for most (e.g., >99%) attacks to succeed. Specifically, we vary the maximum perturbation size of range [0, .05, .1, .15, .2, .25, .3], and visualize the drop in model accuracy on the adversarial examples in Figure 5.3.

## 5.9   RESULT ANALYSIS

The FGSM works by using the gradients of the neural network to create an adversarial example. For an input image, the method uses the gradients of the loss concerning the

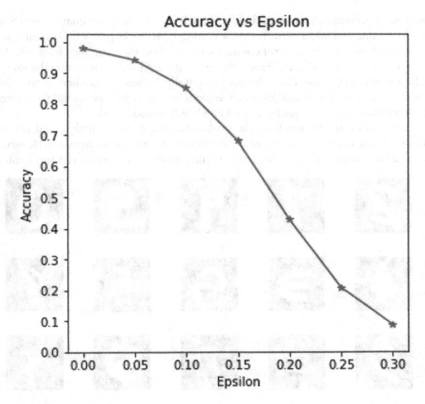

**FIGURE 5.3** Line chart.

input image to create a new image that maximizes the loss. This new image is called the adversarial image. It can be summarized using the following expression:

$$adv\_x=x+\epsilon*sign(\nabla xJ(\theta,x,y))$$

where

- adv_x: Adversarial image.
- x: Original input image.
- y: Original input label.
- $\epsilon$
- : Multiplier to ensure the perturbations are small.
- $\theta$
- : Model parameters.
- J
- : Loss.

An intriguing property here is that the gradients are taken concerning the input image. It is done because the objective is to create an image that maximizes the loss.

A method to accomplish this is to find how much each pixel in the image contributes to the loss value and add a perturbation accordingly. It works pretty fast because it is easy to find how each input pixel contributes to the loss by using the chain rule and finding the required gradients. Hence, the gradients are taken concerning the image. In addition, since the model is no longer being trained (thus, the gradient is not taken concerning the trainable variables, i.e., the model parameters), the model parameters remain constant. The only goal is to fool an already-trained model.

We tried out different epsilon values, observed the resultant image, and noticed that as the value of epsilon increases, it becomes easier to fool the network. However, this comes as a trade-off, resulting in the perturbations becoming more identifiable.

**FIGURE 5.4**  Examples of adversarial samples.

We can see that the greater the value of epsilon, the model learning is degraded and starts to misclassify the digits.

In the end, we plotted several examples of adversarial samples at each epsilon (as shown in Figure 5.4).

## 5.10 SUMMARY

The chapter aims to develop a model to countermeasure the misuse of a deep generative model by utilizing adversarial attacks to create subtle alarms that would cause deep generative algorithms to fail in generating the fake image in the first place. One of the main goals of adversarial attacks on neural networks is misclassification, where we only want to drive the model into making wrong predictions without worrying about the actual class of the prediction; in our experiment, we can see that when the epsilon value is 0 (e=0), training is normal and with every increase in the value of epsilon (e), the model learning is degraded and starts to misclassify the digits eventually.

## REFERENCES

[1] Plangger, K. (2020). DFs: Perspectives on the future "reality" of advertising and branding. International Journal of Advertising. https://doi.org/10.1080/02650 487.2020.1834211

[2] Neekhara, P., Dolhansky, B., Bitton, J., & Ferrer, C. C. (1970, January 1). *Adversarial threats to DF detection: A practical perspective.* CVF Open Access. Retrieved January 11, 2022, from https://openaccess.thecvf.com/content/CVPR2021W/WMF/html/Neekhara_Adversarial_Threats_to_DF_Detection_A_Practical_Perspective_CVPRW_2021_paper.html

[3] Akhtar, N., & Mian, A. (2018). "Threat of Adversarial Attacks on DL in Computer Vision: A Survey," in *IEEE Access*, vol. 6, pp. 14410–14430. doi:10.1109/ACCESS.2018.2807385

[4] Krizhevsky, A., Sutskever, I., & Hinton, G. E. (2012). ImageNet Classification with Deep Convolutional Neural Networks. In F. Pereira, C. J. C. Burges, L. Bottou, & K. Q. Weinberger (Reds), *Advances in Neural Information Processing Systems* (Vol. 25). Opgehaal van, https://proceedings.neurips.cc/paper/2012/file/c399862d3b9d6b76c8436e924a68c45b-Paper.pdf

[5] He, K., Zhang, X., Ren, S., & Sun, J. (2015, February 6). *Delving deep into rectifiers: Surpassing human-level performance on ImageNet classification.* arXiv.org. Retrieved January 11, 2022, from https://arxiv.org/abs/1502.01852

[6] America, R. C. N. E. C. L., Collobert, R., America, N. E. C. L., America, J. W. N. E. C. L., Weston, J., University, C. M., Amherst, U. of M., Google, U. of T. and, & Metrics, O. M. V. A. (2008, July 1). *A unified architecture for natural language processing: Deep Neural Networks with multitask learning.* A unified architecture for natural language processing | Proceedings of the 25th International Conference on ML. Retrieved January 11, 2022, from https://dl.acm.org/doi/10.1145/1390156.1390177

[7] Biggio, B., Corona, I., Maiorca, D., Nelson, B., Srndic, N., Laskov, P., Giacinto, G., & Roli, F. (2017, August 21). *Evasion attacks against ML at test time.* arXiv.org. Retrieved January 11, 2022, from https://arxiv.org/abs/1708.06131

[8]  Szegedy, C., Zaremba, W., Sutskever, I., Bruna, J., Erhan, D., Goodfellow, I., & Fergus, R. (2014, February 19). *Intriguing properties of neural networks.* arXiv.org. Retrieved January 11, 2022, from https://arxiv.org/abs/1312.6199

[9]  Nguyen, A., Yosinski, J., & Clune, J. (2015, April 2). *Deep neural networks are easily fooled: High confidence predictions for unrecognizable images.* arXiv.org. Retrieved January 11, 2022, from https://arxiv.org/abs/1412.1897

[10]  Moosavi-Dezfooli, S.-M., Fawzi, A., & Frossard, P. (2016, July 4). *DeepFool: A simple and accurate method to fool Deep Neural Networks.* arXiv.org. Retrieved January 11, 2022, from https://arxiv.org/abs/1511.04599

[11]  Dong, Y., Liao, F., Pang, T., Su, H., Zhu, J., Hu, X., & Li, J. (1970, January 1). *Boosting adversarial attacks with momentum.* CVF Open Access. Retrieved January 11, 2022, from https://openaccess.thecvf.com/content_cvpr_2018/html/Dong_Boosting_Adversarial_Attacks_CVPR_2018_paper.html

[12]  Madry, A., Makelov, A., Schmidt, L., Tsipras, D., & Vladu, A. (2019, September 4). *Towards DL models resistant to adversarial attacks.* arXiv.org. Retrieved January 10, 2022, from https://arxiv.org/abs/1706.06083

[13]  Goodfellow, I., Pouget-Abadie, J., Mirza, M., Xu, B., WardeFarley, D., Ozair, S., Courville, A., & Bengio, Y. (2014). Generative adversarial nets. In *Advances in Neural Information Processing Systems*, pp. 2672–2680.

[14]  Odena, A., Olah, C., & Shlens, J. (2017, July 20). *Conditional image synthesis with auxiliary classifier Gans.* arXiv.org. Retrieved January 11, 2022, from https://arxiv.org/abs/1610.09585

[15]  Gilmer, J., Ford, N., Carlini, N., & Cubuk, E. (2019, May 24). *Adversarial examples are a natural consequence of test error in noise.* PMLR. Retrieved January 11, 2022, from http://proceedings.mlr.press/v97/gilmer19a.html

[16]  Xiao, C., Zhu, J.-Y., Li, B., He, W., Liu, M., & Song, D. (2018, January 9). *Spatially transformed adversarial examples.* arXiv.org. Retrieved January 11, 2022, from https://arxiv.org/abs/1801.02612

[17]  Zhao, Z., Dua, D., & Singh, S. (2018, February 23). *Generating natural adversarial examples.* arXiv.org. Retrieved January 11, 2022, from https://arxiv.org/abs/1710.11342

[18]  Ruiz, N., Bargal, S. A., & Sclaroff, S. (2020, April 27). *Disrupting DFs: Adversarial attacks against conditional image translation networks and facial manipulation systems.* arXiv.org. Retrieved January 5, 2022, from https://arxiv.org/abs/2003.01279

[19]  Qiu, S., Liu, Q., Zhou, S., & Wu, C. (2019). Review of AI adversarial attack and defense technologies. Applied Sciences, Vol. 9, No. 5, p. 909. MDPI AG. Retrieved from http://dx.doi.org/10.3390/app9050909

[20]  Finlayson, S. G., Chung, H. W., Kohane, I. S., & Beam, A. L. (2019, February 4). *Adversarial attacks against Medical DL systems.* arXiv.org. Retrieved January 6, 2022, from https://arxiv.org/abs/1804.05296

[21]  Samangouei, P., Kabkab, M., & Chellappa, R. (2018, May 18). *Defense-GAN: Protecting classifiers against adversarial attacks using generative models.* arXiv.org. Retrieved January 6, 2022, from https://arxiv.org/abs/1805.06605

[22]  Santhanam, G. K., & Grnarova, P. (2018, May 27). *Defending against adversarial attacks by leveraging an entire GAN.* arXiv.org. Retrieved January 6, 2022, from https://arxiv.org/abs/1805.10652

[23]  Hu, W., & Tan, Y. (2017, February 20). *Generating adversarial malware examples for black-box attacks based on GAN.* arXiv.org. Retrieved January 6, 2022, from https://arxiv.org/abs/1702.05983

[24] Gandhi, A. & S. Jain, "Adversarial Perturbations Fool DF Detectors," *2020 International Joint Conference on Neural Networks (IJCNN)*, 2020, pp. 1–8. doi:10.1109/IJCNN48605.2020.9207034.

[25] Liu, X., & Hsieh, C.-J. (2019, April 15). *Rob-Gan: Generator, discriminator, and adversarial attacker*. arXiv.org. Retrieved January 11, 2022, from https://arxiv.org/abs/1807.10454

[26] Croce, F., & Hein, M. (2019, October). Sparse and imperceivable adversarial attacks. *Proceedings of the IEEE/CVF International Conference on Computer Vision (ICCV)*.

[27] Zhang, H., & Wang, J. (2019). Defense Against Adversarial Attacks Using Feature Scattering-based Adversarial Training. In H. Wallach, H. Larochelle, A. Beygelzimer, F. d'Alché-Buc, E. Fox, & R. Garnett (eds), *Advances in Neural Information Processing Systems* (Vol. 32). Opgehaal van, https://proceedings.neurips.cc/paper/2019/file/d8700cbd38cc9f30cecb34f0c195b137-Paper.pdf

[28] Liao, F., Liang, M., Dong, Y., Pang, T., Hu, X., & Zhu, J. (2018). Defense against Adversarial Attacks Using High-Level Representation Guided Denoiser. *arXiv [cs. CV]*. Opgehaal van, http://arxiv.org/abs/1712.02976

[29] Mustafa, A., Khan, S. H., Hayat, M., Shen, J., & Shao, L. (2020). Image Super-Resolution as a Defense Against Adversarial Attacks. IEEE Transactions on Image Processing, Vol. 29, pp. 1711–1724. doi:10.1109/TIP.2019.2940533

[30] Song, S., Chen, Y., Cheung, N.-M., & Kuo, C.-C. J. (2018). Defense Against Adversarial Attacks with Saak Transform. *arXiv [cs.CV]*. Opgehaal van, http://arxiv.org/abs/1808.01785

[31] Sharma, D. K., Gaur, L., & Okunbor, D. (2007). "Image compression and feature extraction with neural network," Proceedings of the Academy of Information and Management Sciences, 11(1), 33–38.

[32] Anshu, K., Gaur, L., & Khazanchi, D. (2017) "Evaluating satisfaction level of grocery E-retailers using intuitionistic fuzzy TOPSIS and ECCSI model," *International Conference on Infocom Technologies and Unmanned Systems (Trends and Future Directions) (ICTUS)*, pp. 276–284. doi:10.1109/ICTUS.2017.8286019

[33] Gaur, L., & Anshu, K. (2018). Consumer preference analysis for websites using e-TailQ and AHP. International Journal of Engineering & Technology, Vol. 7, No. 2.11, pp. 14–20.

[34] Rana, J., Gaur, L., Singh, G., Awan, U. & Rasheed, M.I. (2021). Reinforcing customer journey through artificial intelligence: A review and research agenda. International Journal of Emerging Markets, Vol. ahead-of-print (No. ahead-of-print). https://doi.org/10.1108/IJOEM-08-2021-1214

[35] Gaur, L., Singh, G., Solanki, A., Jhanjhi, N. Z., Bhatia, U., Sharma, S., ... & Kim, W. (2021), "Disposition of youth in predicting sustainable development goals using the neuro-fuzzy and random forest algorithms" Human-Centric Computing and Information Sciences, 11, NA.

[36] Singh, G., Kumar, B., Gaur, L., & Tyagi, A. (2019). "Comparison between Multinomial and Bernoulli Naïve Bayes for Text Classification," *2019 International Conference on Automation, Computational and Technology Management (ICACTM)*, pp. 593–596. doi:10.1109/ICACTM.2019.8776800

[37] Gaur, L., Agarwal, V., & Anshu, K. (2020). Fuzzy DEMATEL Approach to Identify the Factors Influencing Efficiency of Indian Retail. In P. K. Kapur, O. Singh, S. Khatri, & A. Verma (eds.) *Strategic System Assurance and Business Analytics. Asset Analytics (Performance and Safety Management)*. Springer, Singapore. 69–83. https://doi.org/10.1007/978-981-15-3647-2_

[38] Gaur, L., Afaq, A., Singh, G. & Dwivedi, Y.K. (2021). Role of artificial intelligence and robotics to foster the touchless travel during a pandemic: A review and research agenda. International Journal of Contemporary Hospitality Management, Vol. 33, No. 11, pp. 4079–4098. https://doi.org/10.1108/IJCHM-11-2020-1246

[39] Sharma, S., Singh, G., Gaur, L., & Sharma, R. (2022). Does psychological distance and religiosity influence fraudulent customer behaviour? International Journal of Consumer Studies. doi:10.1111/ijcs.12773

[40] Sahu, G., Gaur, L., & Singh, G. (2021). Applying niche and gratification theory approach to examine the users' indulgence towards over-the-top platforms and conventional TV. Telematics and Informatics, 65. doi:10.1016/j.tele.2021.101713

[41] Ramakrishnan, R., Gaur, L., & Singh, G. (2016). Feasibility and efficacy of BLE beacon IoT devices in inventory management at the shop floor. International Journal of Electrical and Computer Engineering, Vol. 6, No. 5, pp. 2362–2368. doi:10.11591/ijece.v6i5.10807

[42] Afaq, A., Gaur, L., Singh, G., & Dhir, A. (2021). COVID-19: Transforming air passengers' behaviour and reshaping their expectations towards the airline industry. Tourism Recreation Research. doi:10.1080/02508281.2021.2008211

[43] Mahbub, Md. K., Biswas, M., Gaur, L., Alenezi, F., & Santosh, K. (2022). Deep features to detect pulmonary abnormalities in chest X-rays due to infectious disease X: Covid-19, pneumonia, and tuberculosis. Information Sciences, Vol. 592, pp. 389–401. https://doi.org/10.1016/J.INS.2022.01.062

[44] Sharma, S., Singh, G., Gaur, L., & Sharma, R. (2022). Does psychological distance and religiosity influence fraudulent customer behavior? International Journal of Consumer Studies. 10.1111/ijcs.12773.

[45] Zaman, N., & Gaur, L. (2022). Approaches and Applications of Deep Learning in Virtual Medical Care. IGI. doi:10.4018/978-1-7998-8929-8.ch002.

# 6 Detection of DeepFakes Using Local Features and Convolutional Neural Network

*Shreya Rastogi, Amit Kumar Mishra, and Loveleen Gaur*

## CONTENTS

## 6.1 INTRODUCTION

The well-known DeepFake (DF) can quickly generate or change the face of the person in photos and recordings using techniques relying on deep learning (DL) technology. It is one of the fast-growing phenomena [1]. It is feasible to get outstanding outcomes by producing new multimedia items that are difficult to distinguish as actual or artificial to the bare eyes. However, the term DF refers to all audiovisual material that has been synthetically manipulated or generated using ML generative models [2]. Thanks to the new technology, anyone can make a DF from a few photos, so fake movies will extend beyond famous spheres and drive revenge erotica. "DF technology is being weaponized against women," says Danielle Citron, a law professor at Boston University [3]. Concerns about the harmful consequences of DFs have sparked a surge in curiosity in DF recognition [4]. DFs entail morphing one person's visage into that of another in ways that a person editor would not consider or be able to notice [5]. Faces are frequently swapped, or facial expressions are manipulated in DF films, as shown in Figure 6.1. The face here on the left side is exchanged with the

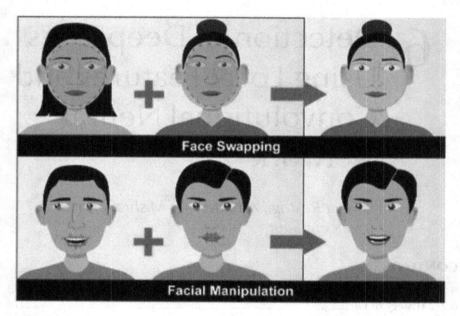

**FIGURE 6.1**    Swapping and manipulation of the face in DF videos [6].

body of some other individual. The features of the left-side face are replicated by the right-side face in facial manipulation [6]. In Figure 6.2, the manipulation in the face of the celebrity is an example of how DF works in real life.

ML is the crucial element of DFs, and it has allowed them to be produced considerably quicker and at a cheaper price [7]. To construct a DF movie of anyone, a developer would, first of all, prepare a neural network on several minutes of actual surveillance video of the person who gives it a realistic "understanding" of how they or appears from various perspectives and light conditions. The neural model would then be combined with visual effects to overlay a replica of the human over another person [8]. Whereas the incorporation of AI speeds up the procedure, it still requires time to create a plausible mixture that sets a human in an imaginary scenario. To prevent glitches and distortions in the picture, the designer must alter several of the properly trained system's settings individually [9]. After the introduction, the history and application of DFs are discussed. It is followed by the advantages and the disadvantages of DF. After that, the generation and the detection techniques of DF are explained.

## 6.2   HISTORY OF DF

Christoph Bregler, Michele Covell, and Malcolm Slaney created the Visual Rewrite Offsite Link software in 1997, which transformed existing video footage of a speaker to reflect the phrases contained in a separate music signal. For the first time, face

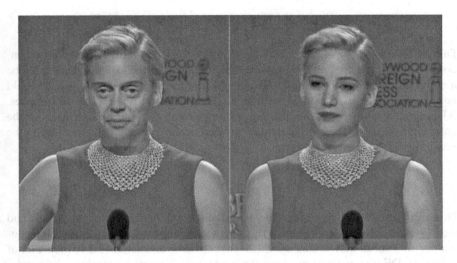

**FIGURE 6.2** The picture on the left side is the original picture, and the picture on the right side has been manufactured using the DF technology [10].

reanimation was completely automated [11]. To achieve this, it used ML techniques to correlate noises made by a movie's protagonist with their head form. The software was created to be used in cinematic transcoding, allowing the performers' facial gestures to be matched to a dynamic theme. Human vision synthesis improved as computer vision and AI matured. Using an ML approach known as a Generative Adversarial Network (GAN), Offsite Link enabled the wider populace to impose the preexisting pictures and movies onto raw photos or videos. DF Offsite Link, a combination of "deep learning" and "fake," was invented in 2017 [12].

## 6.3 APPLICATIONS OF DEEPFAKES

There are various applications of DFs such as the following:

1. Education

DFs can help teachers offer compelling lectures. Furthermore, these lectures would transcend standard graphical and multimedia mediums. In the study, synthetic media developed by AI can indeed bring ancient folks to reality. Classes become more exciting and participatory as a result. A reenactment film or audio and video of a mythological person will also have a more significant effect. It could boost enthusiasm and make teaching highly beneficial. The employment of synthetic speech and video on a global level and reasonably can increase effectiveness and achieve the aim [13].

## 2. Art

DF can make pricey "VFX" technologies more accessible. It may also be a tremendous tool for freelance creators at a substantial fraction of the expense. DFs could be a powerful technique for bringing humor or satire to life in a realistic way. It could be a reenactment, extension, deformation, or exploitation of real-life occurrences. AI-generated synthetic media also has a lot of promise. It can expose doors in the entertainment world. Several individual producers and YouTubers are also using the possibility [14].

## 3. Liberation and autonomy

Human rights advocates and reporters might utilize synthetic media in autocratic and harsh countries to stay anonymous. By using technology to denounce crimes on conventional or social networking sites, citizen journalists and activists may gain a lot of influence. DF is sometimes used to safeguard people's rights by masking their audio and features [13].

## 4. There is no linguistic barrier.

DF is an excellent approach for using AI technology to overcome the language barrier. The iconic advertisement in which David Beckham was shown reciting nine distinct languages to convey a statement for the Malaria Must Die Initiative is an excellent illustration of what DFs can accomplish [14].

## 5. Research

DF technology may also build personalized replicas beyond infotainment and learning. These might then be deployed within apps that let individuals put on numerous garments or haircuts at their ease and specialized learning apps. A few of these fields are medicine, where creative innovation has already been utilized to generate "fake" neuroimaging based on actual patient data. These fictitious images are being used to build programs that detect tumors in real-world pictures [15].

## 6. Monetary savings

Some argue that creative innovation offers a remarkable ability to revolutionize various sectors. Generic technology might help people and businesses to enter these industries with less expenditure by allowing for the low-cost development of everything from films to advertisements and games.

The innovation is not as harmful as the future applications. If organizations that employ DF technology are held to high ethical standards and dangerous applications are effectively avoided, this technology has a lot of potential.

## 6.4 ADVANTAGES OF DEEPFAKE

There are various advantages of DFs such as:

1. Allows worldwide ads to be adjusted and "translated exactly" for native dialects and brand names.
2. Enhances private processes by allowing directors to communicate with their employees worldwide in the ideal native dialect.
3. One can act in a movie even if they die in real life.
4. Make a film using a younger version of yourself or another performer in the lead role [16,17].

## 6.5 DISADVANTAGES OF DEEPFAKE

There are various disadvantages of DFs such as:

1. Deception at the management level

DF attacks are the most popular type of attack. Counterfeiters no more attempt to convince a company member to wire funds via forged email. They persuade them with a telephone conversation from someone who seems much like a financial officer or director.

2 Coercion of funds from companies or consumers

Faces and sounds copied to media files using DF reveal individuals making bogus remarks. It is easy to record a CEO delivering fictitious pronouncements. Deliberately provoking them to leak the film to press agencies or broadcast it on social media might potentially be used to coerce a firm.

3. Pessimistic viewers will not accept or appreciate any information or proof caught on film or television.
4. Take control of one biometrics

## 6.6 DEEPFAKES GENERATION

Generation of DF can be performed with the use of these techniques:

1. Using a GAN

GANs are used to construct DFs. They appear to be so convincing because a GAN framework's sole purpose is to build one that can deceive it into trusting its legitimacy. As shown in Figure 6.3, a generation in the architecture creates the pictures, and afterward, the discriminator checks out discrepancies. The generator understands whatever the discriminator doesn't seem like and changes to make a significantly better counterfeit using ML [18].

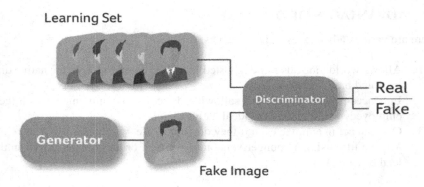

Learning Set

Discriminator — Real / Fake

Generator

Fake Image

**FIGURE 6.3**   Working of GAN [18].

2.  Using Autoencoder

The capacity of DL to represent complicated and high-dimensional information is well known [19]. Deep autoencoders, a type of deep network having such capacity, have been widely used for dimensionality reduction and compression of the picture [20].

Yuezun Li et al. [21], in their study, explained a generation technique of the DF. Figure 6.4 depicts the complete workflow of the simple DF generation. Faces of the subject are recognized in an incoming clip, and feature points are collected subsequently. The landmarks are utilized to coordinate the features in a consistent pattern. The affiliated features then were resized and sent through an autoencoder to create contributor pictures with almost the same emotional expressions as the original user's features. The autoencoder is typically made up of two Convolutional Neural Networks (CNNs): an "encoder" and a "decoder." The encoder E turns the face of the source target into a code vector. There is just one "encoder" to ensure that identity-independent features, including visual gestures, are captured irrespective of the individuals' identities sets. Each identity has its decoder, "Di," that uses the code to construct the person's visage. In an unsupervised approach, the encoder and decoder were properly trained together, utilizing unrelated picture collections of many individuals.

In particular, as shown in Figure 6.5, an encoder-decoder pair is generated using "E" and "Di" for each subject's input visage, and their features are optimized to minimize rebuilding errors (L1 difference between the source and rebuilt appearances). Back-propagation is used to adjust the parameters until saturation is achieved. Therefore, the synthetic features are twisted back to the initial user's facial arrangement and clipped again from the feature point with a filter. The final phase minimizes the transitions seen between synthetic and actual frames. The entire process can be automated and requires very little human participation.

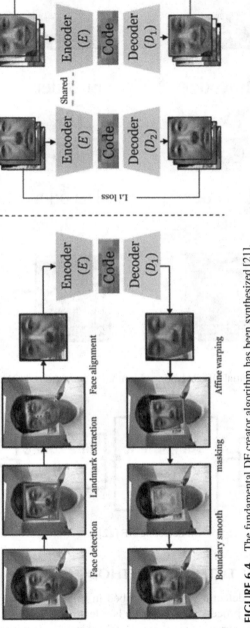

**FIGURE 6.4** The fundamental DF creator algorithm has been synthesized [21].

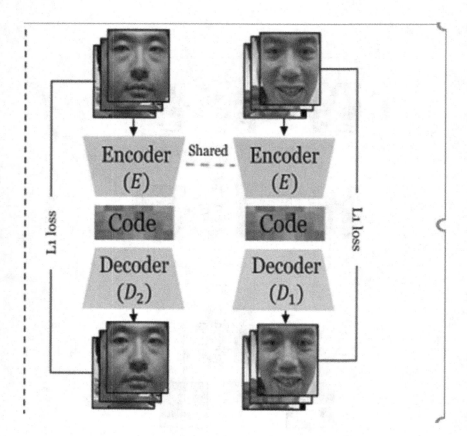

**FIGURE 6.5**    The initial DF generating algorithm is being trained [21].

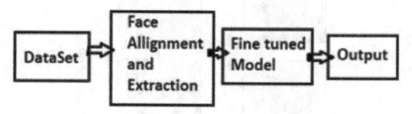

**FIGURE 6.6**    The basic flow for detecting DF [22].

## 6.7   DEEPFAKES DETECTION METHODS

The basic flow for detecting DF is described in Figure 6.6. There are four steps involved in the whole process. The first step is selecting the dataset. In the second step, face alignment and extraction are done. The third step deals with applying a model to detect the DF. Moreover, in the last step, the output is defined.

Different methods for detecting the DFs are described in the following:

1. DF Detection Using Biological Signals

One of the methods of detecting DF is biological signals. In this method, biological signals are extracted from both the input or actual data and fake ones. Then, signal transformation is applied to calculate spatial coherence and temporal consistency. Furthermore, feature vectors are created, and classifiers are used to calculate the authenticity [23].

2. DF Detection Using Phoneme-Viseme Mismatches

This method uses the concept "visemes," which describe the movements of the jaw structure, which might be distinct or contradictory from the spoken morpheme. For example, there may be a morpheme discrepancy when pronouncing phrases such as mama, baba, and papa, which may be utilized to identify even modest geographically and statistically restricted changes in DF films [24].

3. DFs Detection Using Convolutional Neural Network

One of the methods to detect the DF is by using CNN. Karandikar [25], as shown in Figure 6.7, have described a model for detecting the DF. In this model, CNN is a binary classifier with four convolutional layers. This model removes steadily reduced noise signals by applying the same picture level preprocessing to both actual and false pictures. Enabling the forensics models to understand extra inherent features to identify the produced and actual feature photos.

Apart from this model, there are various models where CNN is used in detecting the DF; for example, Montserrat et al. [26] have developed the model to detect the DF, and in this model, CNN is used to extract the facial features from the face. Rana

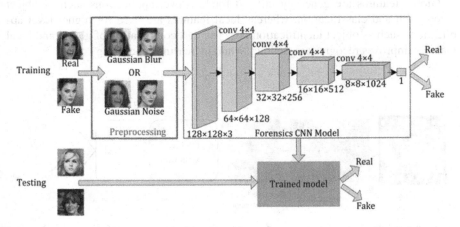

**FIGURE 6.7**   Detection of DF using CNN [25].

and Sung [27] have proposed a model called "DFStack" that used CNN as a classi-fier to detect DF. Shad et al. [28] have presented a comparative study on the models for detecting DF using CNN. In his research, different datasets are used to train eight different CNNs. Ahmed and Sonuç [29] have presented a DF detection model using CNN on the MATLAB platform. The summary of other DF detection models is ex-plained in Table 6.1.

## 6.8  LOCAL AND GLOBAL FEATURES OF THE IMAGE

The information collected from pictures in numeric figures that seem to be challen-ging to humans to grasp and interpret is known as features. Assuming that the image represents information, the information collected from the statistics is called features. The dimensions of features retrieved from a picture are usually substantially smaller than the actual photograph. The expenses of analyzing the group of photos are re-duced due to the dimensionality reduction.

In general, two types of features are retrieved from photos depending on the usage. These are local and global features. Descriptors are a term used to describe features. Local descriptors are utilized for item acknowledgment, whereas global descriptors are used for picture extraction, object recognition, and categorization. The distinc-tion between detection and characterization is significant. Detection is the process of determining the presence of a thing (e.g., determining if an object exists in a picture or movie). At the same time, recognition is the process of selecting an entity's identity (e.g., recognizing an individual) [39].

Local features represent the image portions (critical locations in the picture) of an item, while global features represent the picture as a complete to describe the whole thing. Contour representations, form identifiers, and texture features are global features, whereas local features represent the structure in an image portion. Global descriptors include "Shape Matrices," "Histogram Oriented Gradients (HOG)," and "Co-HOG." Local descriptors include "SIFT," "SURF," "LBP," "BRISK," and "FREAK" [27].

Global features are generally utilized for low-level applications such as object recognition and classification, whereas local features are used for higher-level ap-plications such as object identification. The use of a combination of global and local features improves recognition accuracy while increasing processing costs.

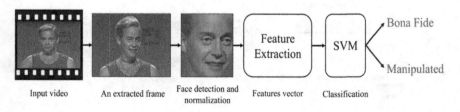

Input video        An extracted frame    Face detection and    Features vector    Classification
                                         normalization

**FIGURE 6.8**   The flow of detection of face DF using local features [41].

**TABLE 6.1**
**Summary of DF Detection Model Using "CNN"**

| Author | Year | Key Finding | Accuracy | Limitation/Future Work |
|---|---|---|---|---|
| Li and Lyu [30] | 2018 | Developed the CNN-based algorithm to detect the DF. The strategy is predicated on the notion that the present DF algorithm produces only pictures with restricted resolutions. Therefore, this must be progressively altered to match the features in the data record. | AUC performance on the UADFV dataset is 97.4, and on "DFTIMIT" LQ is 99.9 | Improvement in the robustness of the detection algorithm. |
| Guera and Delp [31] | 2019 | They offered a "temporal-aware" process for detecting DF films autonomously. Used "CNN" for extracting features (frame level). Used RNN to train the model to find whether or not a video has been manipulated. | Training accuracy for 20 frames: 99.5%. Validation accuracy: 96.9 Test accuracy: 96.7 | To investigate the ways to improve the algorithm's robustness against edited films by employing previously unexplored strategies during the training phase. |
| Sohrawardi et al. [32] | 2019 | The paper aims to tackle the issues from a reporter's point of view and work effectively at designing a device that would blend in effortlessly. Proposed a method that will let viewers identify whether or not a video shared on the internet is a DF securely and effectively. | Equal error rate for "ResNeXTSpoof": 5.4% Equal error rate for "convolutional LSTM": 6.4% | To conduct live beta testing, allowing a more extensive amount of people to attend. |
| Irene Amerini et al. [33] | 2019 | ->Provided a novel forensic strategy for distinguishing between false and authentic surveillance videos, contrary to the previous techniques that rely on single frames. ->They used optical flow fields to investigate probable interframe dissimilarities. | Accuracy of "VGG16": 81.61% | To evaluate the algorithm's accuracy by using different datasets and neural networks. |
| Hua Qi et al. [34] | 2020 | ->Proposed a model named "DeepRhythm" for the detection of DF by tracking heartbeat rhythms. ->Systems adapts to constantly evolving face and false kinds by using dual-spatial-temporal attention. | Accuracy: 0.98 | To use the proposed model in other fields like combatting non-traditional adversarial attacks. |

*(continued)*

**TABLE 6.1 (Continued)**
**Summary of DF Detection Model Using "CNN"**

| Author | Year | Key Finding | Accuracy | Limitation/Future Work |
|---|---|---|---|---|
| Gandhi and Jain [35] | 2020 | -> In both black box and white box situations, adversarial perturbations were made using the "Fast Gradient Sign Method" and "the Carlin" and "Wagner L2" norm attack.<br>->Unsupervised generative CNN is used in the DIP. | Accuracy: 98% | Not mentioned |
| Wang et al. [36] | 2020 | -> Study shows that with proper processing and data augmentation, a typical picture detector trained on only one CNN generator may generalize unexpectedly well to previously unexplored structures, datasets, and training methodologies.<br>->Suggested the fascinating idea that CNN-generated photos have some common systemic defects that prohibit them from obtaining high quality. | Accuracy: 98.2 | Not mentioned |
| Tarasiou et al. [43] | 2020 | ->Presented "Celeb-DF," an innovative vast problematic DF video dataset with 5,639 high-quality DF films of superstars developed using an enhanced synthesis approach.<br>->Thorough examination of DF detection methods and data to highlight the increased level of difficulty offered by Celeb-DF. | "Xception-c40" gives the AUC score of 65.5 on the "Celeb-DF" dataset. | Celeb-DF should include anti-forensic methods. |
| Zi et al. [37] | 2020 | ->Proposed "WildDF," a new dataset that contains 7,314 facial patterns derived from 707 DF films obtained entirely from the web.<br>->Performed a comprehensive analysis of a set of baseline detection systems. | Sequence-level detection accuracy: 65.50% | Not mentioned |
| Li et al. [38] | 2020 | ->Presented a unique Patch Pair Convolutional Neural Networks (PPCNN) method for distinguishing DF movies or pictures from the real stuff. | AUC score on "Faceforensics C0": 99.4 | To create a broader model to recognize complicated DFs with varying compression and pixel density. |

**TABLE 6.2**
**Summary of DF Detection Using "Local Features" of the Image**

| Author | Year | Key findings | Accuracy | Future work/Limitation |
|---|---|---|---|---|
| Akhtar and Dasgupta. [42] | 2019 | It is proposed that the significant characteristic for the automated identification of modified facial photographs is the use of local image characteristics that are common across the manipulated areas. <br> -> Create a compact framework with the appropriate architectural constraints for retrieving these features. <br> ->Develop a multifunctional training approach that beats picture class supervision individually constantly. | Accuracy: 98.03 | Not mentioned |
| Agarwal et al. [44] | 2021 | -> Present the "Weighted Local Magnitude Pattern (WLMP)," a unique and operationally intensive pattern classifier that tries to encapsulate the invisible distortions that are contained in photos after digital alteration. <br> -> By using the existing "WLMP classifier," proposed a unique "MagNet" method for efficiently distinguishing among digitized briefing assaults and authentic non-tampered video files. | Accuracy on "FaceForensics" database: 100% | The presented algorithm's effectiveness can be enhanced in cross-attack scenarios. |
| Kawa et al. [45] | 2020 | -> Developed and tested a new activation function "Pish" that allows with even better reliability at the price of minor time resources. <br> ->Show initial findings of a DeepFake detection approach premised on "Local Feature Descriptors," which enables the platform to be set up considerably quicker as well as instead of the use of GPUs. | Error rate: 0.28 | To obtain a reduced EER, the goal is to extend the LFD-based approaches. |
| Abdullah et al. [46] | 2020 | -> Suggested a new method for determining ECG beat categorization. The suggested method relies on image analysis. <br> -> ECG pulse snaps are first stored as ECG pulse pictures, and then feature collection from ECG pulse pictures is done using local feature descriptors. | Accuracy: 99.9% | ->The feature selection method and the combination of local descriptors will be examined. <br> ->To utilize other ML techniques in the proposed architecture. |
| Wang et al. [47] | 2021 | -> "FFR_FD" is proposed as an insightful vector to express the face 'image definition, which is built using local feature descriptors via segmented face areas. | AUC score on "DFTIMIT" LQ- 99.9 | -> To create a facial forensics exclusionary characteristic identifier. |

### 6.8.1 DeepFakes Detection Using Local Features

The pixel-based extraction of features approaches is used in the local feature-based DF detection. It extracts the characteristics from every pixel. Local feature-based detection has better efficiency than visual feature-based detection because it captures all parts of the visage. The resultant features are inherent and usually not visible to the naked eye [40].

Detection of "face" DFs is often seen as a binary classification problem, in which the source data must be classified as modified or innocuous. The procedure's primary goal is to obtain a unique set of characteristics that, when combined with a classification method, increases the possibility of the source data being realistic. K. N. Ramadhani and R. Munir [41] proposed a flow of system shown in Figure 6.8 to detect the DF using local descriptors. The architecture begins by extracting a single image from a detected visage clip. The visage is then identified by using the "Viola-Jones" method. The visage is adjusted, and characteristics are retrieved using a local image descriptor. The collected features are placed into an SVM classifier, determining whether the data are altered (DF) or genuine. The summary of DF detection models that have been used to detect the DF using local features of the image is presented in Table 6.2.

## 6.9 SUMMARY

The motive of this chapter is to give new researchers a straightforward and brief overview of DF creation and extraction using "local features" and "CNN." It introduces the DFs, their applications, along with the advantages and disadvantages. The most frequently used techniques for the creation of DF are also discussed. Furthermore, the overview of DF detection techniques is explained, along with a summary of the work done in that field (methods). The main techniques described here are detecting DF using "local features" and "CNN."

## REFERENCES

[1]  T. T. Nguyen, Q. V. H. Nguyen, C. M. Nguyen, D. Nguyen, D. T. Nguyen, and S. Nahavandi, "DL for DFs Creation and Detection: A Survey," pp. 1–16, 2019. [Online]. Available: http://arxiv.org/abs/1909.11573.

[2]  J. Kietzmann, L. W. Lee, I. P. McCarthy, and T. C. Kietzmann, "DFs: Trick or Treat?," *Bus. Horiz.*, vol. 63, no. 2, pp. 135–146, 2020, doi:https://doi.org/10.1016/j.bus hor.2019.11.006

[3]  "What Is DF and How Is It Fooling People? – Skeptikai," *Skeptikai – Covering Geo Political, Psychology, Language and More*, 2022. [Online]. Available: https://skepti kai.com/what-is-DF-and-how-is-it-fooling-people/. [Accessed: 02 January 2022].

[4]  G. Shao, 2022. [Online]. Available: www.cnbc.com/2019/10/14/what-is-DF-and-how-it-might-be-dangerous.html. [Accessed: 02 January 2022].

[5]  T. Biggs and R. Moran, "What Is a Deep Fake and How Are They Made?" Smh.com. au, 2022. [Online]. Available: www.smh.com.au/technology/what-is-the-difference-between-a-fake-and-a-DF-20200729-p55ghi.html. [Accessed: 02 January 2022].

[6]  "Deconstructing DFs—How do they work and what are the risks?" *WatchBlog*, 2022.

[7] H. S. Shad et al., "Comparative Analysis of DF Image Detection Method Using Convolutional Neural Network.," *Comput. Intell. Neurosci.*, vol. 2021, p. 3111676, 2021, doi:10.1155/2021/3111676

[8] M. Westerlund, "The Emergence of DF Technology: A Review," *Technol. Innov. Manag. Rev.*, vol. 9, pp. 40–53, 2019, doi:http://doi.org/10.22215/timreview/1282

[9] S. Adee, "What Are DFs and How Are They Created?" *IEEE Spectrum*, 2022. [Online]. Available: https://spectrum.ieee.org/what-is-DF. [Accessed: 14 January 2022].

[10] R. Gonzales, "DFs: How to Tell What's Real When Nothing Is," *GIANT FREAKIN ROBOT*, 2022. [Online]. Available: www.giantfreakinrobot.com/tech/DFs.html. [Accessed: 2 January 2022].

[11] D. Song, "A Short History of DFs," *Medium*, 2022. [Online]. Available: https://medium.com/@songda/a-short-history-of-DFs-604ac7be6016. [Accessed: 4 January 2022].

[12] R. Toews, "DFs Are Going to Wreak Havoc on Society. We Are Not Prepared," *Forbes*, 2022. [Online]. Available: www.forbes.com/sites/robtoews/2020/05/25/DFs-are-going-to-wreak-havoc-on-society-we-are-not-prepared/?sh=60ac43bb7494. [Accessed: 4 January 2022].

[13] A. Jaiman, "Positive Use Cases of DFs," *Medium*, 2022. [Online]. Available: https://towardsdatascience.com/positive-use-cases-of-DFs-49f510056387. [Accessed: 4 January 2022].

[14] Technology.org, 2022. [Online]. Available: www.technology.org/2021/11/26/DF-in-cinematography/. [Accessed: 4 January 2022].

[15] "These Applications of DF Technology Will Amaze You!! – AI School of India," *AI School of India*, 2022. [Online]. Available: https://aischoolofindia.com/parents/these-applications-of-DF-technology-will-amaze-you/. [Accessed: 4 January 2022].

[16] "Pros and Cons: DF Technology and AI Avatars – Springwise," *Springwise*, 2022. [Online]. Available: www.springwise.com/pros-cons/DF-technology-ai-avatars. [Accessed: 4 January 2022].

[17] "Deep Fake / Synthetic Media in Marketing – Advans & Disadvans – PR Smith," PR Smith, 2022. [Online]. Available: https://prsmith.org/2021/10/14/deep-fake-synthetic-media-in-marketing-advans-disadvans/. [Accessed: 6 January 2022].

[18] "DFs Are the New Fake News | Top Business Tech," *Top Business Tech*, 2022. [Online]. Available: https://tbtech.co/news/DFs-are-the-new-fake-news/. [Accessed: 14 January 2022].

[19] A. Voulodimos, N. Doulamis, A. Doulamis, and E. Protopapadakis, "DL for Computer Vision: A Brief Review," *Comput. Intell. Neurosci.*, vol. 2018, pp. 1–14, 2018, doi:10.1155/2018/7068349

[20] B. U. Mahmud and A. Sharmin, "Deep Insights of DF Technology: A Review," vol. 5, pp. 13–23, 2021. [Online]. Available: http://arxiv.org/abs/2105.00192.

[21] Y. Li, X. Yang, P. Sun, H. Qi, and S. Lyu, "Celeb-DF: A Large-Scale Challenging Dataset for DF Forensics," *Proc. IEEE Comput. Soc. Conf. Comput. Vis. Pattern Recognit.*, pp. 3204–3213, 2020, doi:10.1109/CVPR42600.2020.00327

[22] A. Karandikar, "DF Video Detection Using Convolutional Neural Network," *Int. J. Adv. Trends Comput. Sci. Eng.*, vol. 9, no. 2, pp. 1311–1315, 2020, doi:10.30534/ijatcse/2020/62922020

[23] U. A. Ciftci, I. Demir, and L. Yin, "FakeCatcher: Detection of Synthetic Portrait Videos Using Biological Signals," *IEEE Trans. Pattern Anal. Mach. Intell.*, vol. X, no. X, pp. 1–1, 2020, doi:10.1109/tpami.2020.3009287

[24] S. Agarwal, H. Farid, O. Fried, and M. Agrawala, "Detecting Deep-Fake Videos from Phoneme-Viseme Mismatches," 2020 IEEE/CVF Conference on Computer Vision and Pattern Recognition Workshops (CVPRW), 2020, pp. 2814–2822, doi:10.1109/CVPRW50498.2020.00338

[25] A. Karandikar, "DF Video Detection Using Convolutional Neural Network," *Int. J. Adv. Trends Comput. Sci. Eng.*, vol. 9, no. 2, pp. 1311–1315, 2020, doi:10.30534/ijatcse/2020/62922020

[26] D. M. Montserrat et al., "DFs Detection with Automatic Face Weighting," *IEEE Comput. Soc. Conf. Comput. Vis. Pattern Recognit. Work.*, vol. 2020 June, pp. 2851–2859, 2020, doi:10.1109/CVPRW50498.2020.00342

[27] M. S. Rana and A. H. Sung, "DFStack: A Deep Ensemble-based Learning Technique for DF Detection," *Proc. – 2020 7th IEEE Int. Conf. Cyber Secur. Cloud Comput. 2020 6th IEEE Int. Conf. Edge Comput. Scalable Cloud, CSCloud-EdgeCom 2020*, no. August, pp. 70–75, 2020, doi:10.1109/CSCloud-EdgeCom49738.2020.00021

[28] H. S. Shad et al., "Comparative Analysis of DF Image Detection Method Using Convolutional Neural Network," vol. 2021, 2021.

[29] S. R. A. Ahmed and E. Sonuç, "DF Detection Using Rationale-Augmented Convolutional Neural Network," *Appl. Nanosci.*, no. September, 2021, doi:10.1007/s13204-021-02072-3

[30] Y. Li and S. Lyu, "Exposing DF Videos By Detecting Face Warping Artifacts," 2018. [Online]. Available: http://arxiv.org/abs/1811.00656

[31] D. Guera and E. J. Delp, "DF Video Detection Using Recurrent Neural Networks," *Proc. AVSS 2018–2018 15th IEEE Int. Conf. Adv. Video Signal-Based Surveill.*, 2019, doi:10.1109/AVSS.2018.8639163

[32] S. J. Sohrawardi et al., "Poster: Towards Robust Open-world Detection of DFs," *Proc. ACM Conf. Comput. Commun. Secur.*, no. February 2020, pp. 2613–2615, 2019, doi:10.1145/3319535.3363269

[33] Irene Amerini et al., "DF Video Detection through Optical Flow Based CNN Anonymous ICCV Submission," *ICCV Work.*, no. Micc, pp. 1–3, 2019. [Online]. Available: http://openaccess.thecvf.com/content_ICCVW_2019/html/HBU/Amerini_DF_Video_Detection_through_Optical_Flow_Based_CNN_ICCVW_2019_paper.html.

[34] H. Qi et al., "DeepRhythm: Exposing DFs with Attentional Visual Heartbeat Rhythms," *MM 2020 – Proc. 28th ACM Int. Conf. Multimed.*, pp. 1318–1327, 2020, doi:10.1145/3394171.3413707

[35] A. Gandhi and S. Jain, "Adversarial Perturbations Fool DF Detectors," *Proc. Int. Jt. Conf. Neural Networks*, no. Ijcnn, 2020, doi:10.1109/IJCNN48605.2020.9207034

[36] S. Y. Wang, O. Wang, R. Zhang, A. Owens, and A. A. Efros, "CNN-Generated Images Are Surprisingly Easy to Spot. For Now," *Proc. IEEE Comput. Soc. Conf. Comput. Vis. Pattern Recognit.*, pp. 8692–8701, 2020, doi:10.1109/CVPR42600.2020.00872

[37] B. Zi, M. Chang, J. Chen, X. Ma, and Y. G. Jiang, "WildDF: A Challenging Real-World Dataset for DF Detection," *MM 2020 – Proc. 28th ACM Int. Conf. Multimed.*, pp. 2382–2390, 2020, doi:10.1145/3394171.3413769

[38] X. Li, K. Yu, S. Ji, Y. Wang, C. Wu, and H. Xue, "Fighting Against DF: Patch&Pair Convolutional Neural Networks (PPCNN)," *Web Conf. 2020 – Companion World Wide Web Conf. WWW 2020*, no. October, pp. 88–89, 2020, doi:10.1145/3366424.3382711

[39] D. Tyagi, "Introduction to Feature Detection And Matching," *Medium*, 2022. [Online]. Available: https://medium.com/data-breach/introduction-to-feature-detection-and-matching-65e27179885d. [Accessed: 14 January 2022].

[40] A. I. Awad and M. Hassaballah, *Image Feature Detectors and Descriptors*, vol. 630, no. October 2017, Springer, 2016.

[41] K. N. Ramadhani and R. Munir, "A Comparative Study of DF Video Detection Method," *2020 3rd Int. Conf. Inf. Commun. Technol. ICOIACT 2020*, pp. 394–399, 2020, doi:10.1109/ICOIACT50329.2020.9331963

[42] Z. Akhtar and D. Dasgupta, "A Comparative Evaluation of Local Feature Descriptors for DFs Detection," *2019 IEEE Int. Symp. Technol. Homel. Secur. HST 2019*, pp. 0–4, 2019, doi:10.1109/HST47167.2019.9033005

[43] M. Tarasiou and S. Zafeiriou, "Extracting Deep Local Features to Detect Manipulated Images of Human Faces," *Proc. – Int. Conf. Image Process. ICIP*, vol. 2020 October, pp. 1821–1825, 2020, doi:10.1109/ICIP40778.2020.9190714

[44] A. Agarwal, R. Singh, M. Vatsa, and A. Noore, "MagNet: Detecting Digital Presentation Attacks on Face Recognition," *Front. Artif. Intell.*, vol. 4, no. December, pp. 1–19, 2021, doi:10.3389/frai.2021.643424

[45] P. Kawa and P. Syga, "A Note on DF Detection with Low-Resources," 2020. [Online]. Available: http://arxiv.org/abs/2006.05183.

[46] D. A. Abdullah, M. H. Akpınar, and A. Şengür, "Local Feature Descriptors Based ECG Beat Classification," *Heal. Inf. Sci. Syst.*, vol. 8, no. 1, 2020, doi:10.1007/s13755-020-00110-y

[47] G. Wang, Q. Jiang, X. Jin, and X. Cui, "FFR_FD: Effective and Fast Detection of DFs Based on Feature Point Defects," 2021. [Online]. Available: http://arxiv.org/abs/2107.02016.

# 7 DeepFakes
## Positive Cases

### Loveleen Gaur and Gursimar Kaur Arora

## CONTENTS

## 7.1 INTRODUCTION

DeepFakes (DFs) are synthetic media created using DL algorithms, as discussed in the previous chapters. It is essential that further research is conducted on showcasing its positive applications, even if the question of its existence being a bane is still in progress [1]. Godull et al. [2] showcase relevant study stands at 37 out of which about 6 are focused on opportunities related to DF and 13 on its risks. Thus, in the following sections, we discuss how DFs can help the society using various industries as different cases under broader categories of research, content creation, creativity, and strategy in industries such as healthcare and pharma, fashion, retail, E-commerce, media, entertainment, and so forth. After each industry, a table will summarize the cases included along with the technique and its utilization.

DOI: 10.1201/9781003231493-7

## 7.2   APPLICATIONS OF DEEPFAKES

### 7.2.1   Industry: Healthcare and Pharma

#### 7.2.1.1   Case 1

Research is the backbone of the healthcare and pharma industry. Any research in this industry is a possible treatment for life-threatening diseases, drug discovery, or epidemiology. Data collection and data availability have been a point of a hindrance for medical researchers, as it is costly and time-consuming. Zhu et al. proposed a study on using DFs to protect the identity of patients, using the face-swapping technique, and retaining the critical point of the face and body. This method can be a breakthrough in medical research, as the data of patients can be shared with no privacy issues [3]. Synthetic data in terms of healthcare is data generated (medGAN) [4] from training the algorithm on a natural source. This data has various applications, such as detection of tumors, by feeding in X-rays of previously tumor-ridden patients. The other use is extensive research by synthetically creating X-rays. For example, Zhao et al. [5] created real-looking retinal images, using GAN to encourage research in applications of neuronal imaging. Synthetic data can be used to generate sound datasets and pliancy for models of AI [6]. The compatibility with the model is an essential aspect in approving the data by clinical regulations. This data can be helpful in current digital transformations in healthcare [7].

#### 7.2.1.2   Case 2

To facilitate research, rats and rodents are commonly used to test new drugs or find extensive information about some bacteria virus or cells. Leveraging the model DL technology, Coffey et al. [8] have presented their research analysis of Ultrasonic Vocalization (USV) to comprehend better the psychological state and the neural functioning of the animal used during the laboratory testing phase. The model thus created using regional CNN algorithm can convert the audio signals to visual format such as images. This research will have a significant impact by providing in-depth analysis [9,10].

#### 7.2.1.3   Case 3

Apart from research, DFs can now voice those ridden with Motor Neuron Disease (MND). Unfortunately, the patient with this disorder loses the ability to speak, as it affects the spinal cord and brain nerves, which directs our brain to communicate. In its R2 Data Labs, Rolls Royce conglomerated with MND Association, Microsoft, Accenture, Computacenter, Intel, and Dell Technologies [11] to create Quips. It is a voice banking technology where the voice is stored in the voice bank until the MND patients cannot speak. Through the collected voices, synthetic voice is generated with the same voice of the patient. The work of Quip is to hear the conversation and suggest patient responses to choose from without the person to type.

Another software providing voice bank using this cutting-edge technology is VocaliD, which also offers voice capsule and vocal legacy. A voice capsule or audio biography can be defined as a site where a person can record their voice by narrating their stories and experiences and save it for the future generation after buying a voice capsule. Vocal legacy is an indirect method of insuring one's voice by generating digital voice individual to each person, specifically for those who suffer from MND or amyotrophic lateral sclerosis (AML).

| Application/Software/ Program of Study | Use Case | Technique | Website, if any |
|---|---|---|---|
| Zhu et al. [3] | Protecting the privacy of patients | Face Swapping | |
| Coffey et al. [8] | In-depth research and analysis | Analysis of Ultrasonic Vocalization using CNN by converting audio signals to a visual format | |
| Quips [11] | Voice Bank | Audio Synthesis | |
| VocaliD | Voice Bank, Voice Capsule, Vocal Legacy | Audio Synthesis | https://vocalid.ai/ |
| Zhao et al. [5] | Synthetic retinal images to encourage research in neuronal imaging | GAN | |

## 7.2.2 INDUSTRY: RETAIL, E-COMMERCE, CONSULTING

### 7.2.2.1 Case 4

Retail and E-commerce are always on the lookout for better methods for consumer engagement. Synthetic media provides a more straightforward, cheaper, faster, and more effective strategy [12]. As seen in the previous chapters, DFs are not just image or video manipulation but also audio manipulation [13,14,15].

Synthesia, an AI firm from London, has created the software to select an AI Presenter, type in the text that the selected avatar will speak, and voila! Corporate companies have already used this software to create training videos, which can be changed, updated, and even conveyed in different languages—being able to translate plays a massive advantage for multinational firms spread across the globe but have faced the barrier of language, especially when hiring the local citizens. It also created a video with different languages to create awareness for malaria to feature David Beckham; thus, DF is a great tool to create awareness amongst the public.

| Application/Software/ Program of Study | Use Case | Technique | Website, if any |
|---|---|---|---|
| Synthesia | Training videos for corporate | Image generation and audio synthesis | www.synthesia.io/ |

### 7.2.3  INDUSTRY: FASHION

#### 7.2.3.1  Case 5

Originality and vision drive the fashion industry. DFs can create new prints and designs through GAN by training the algorithm on the present methods. DFs also add the element of personalization. Since there is a considerable shift to buying on E-commerce sites, one major disadvantage was imagining oneself in that apparel. Thus, through DFs, one can personalize the model on screen according to one's body dimension, color, and hair type before buying. This application has been implemented in Superpersonal app, a British company [9,10,16,17,18,19].

#### 7.2.3.2  Case 6

A Japanese company, DataGrid, created life-like DFs of fashion models using the GAN technique and further researched motion generation through AI [15,20,21,22,23]. If digital models are implemented, it can be an economical alternate for this industry and efficient. According to Forbes research on market and customers, it was deduced that digital models could reduce cost up to 75% of the price spent on the shooting of products [24].

| Application/Software/ Program of study | Use case | Technique | Website, if any |
| --- | --- | --- | --- |
| Superpersonal [16] | Personalization for online shoppers | Image Generation | www.superpersonal.com/ |
| DataGrid [24] | Digital models | GAN | https://datagrid.co.jp/en/ |

### 7.2.4  INDUSTRY: MEDIA AND ENTERTAINMENT

#### 7.2.4.1  Case 7

This industry is expected to profit the most with the generation of DFs. The DF applications for the media and entertainment industry can be explained through the example of making and broadcasting a film or a video. With the advent of DFs, re-takes won't be bothersome and are primarily reduced in number. The scenes can be manipulated with DF of the scene artists. Also, computer-generated imagery (CGI) is quite expensive, which has led to some of the big banner movies having had the sub-standard effects created by computers. Thus, DFs add the aspect of financial savings for this industry. This can be seen where a DF of South Korean journalists was made to present that day's news; the public was informed of it in advance [13,14,25,26,27].

#### 7.2.4.2  Case 8

When the films are released worldwide, the dubbing needs to be done. But the sound and mouth movement is not in synchronization, and the voice of the actors doesn't sound good enough. It reduces the whole experience of watching a movie. However, with DFs, the audios and videos can be synthesized, and the voice would remain the same as the original actor and the lip sync. TrueSync, a product of Flawless, is a game changer in the art of dubbing by giving quality results for lip-syncing videos. Another innovator using the technology of audio synthesis is Marvel.ai by Veritone, providing Voice as a Service (VaaS) to create and direct synthetic voice and easily personalize it concerning gender, accents, or language. This application has multiple use cases, such as marketing techniques to create creative advertisements and target a larger audience. A media company can use this to convert text to audio, and by the government and public houses for enhanced communication in different languages or dialects and to fabricate interesting e-learning content.

### 7.2.4.3 Case 9

Deep Nostalgia, an AI service by MyHeritage founded by Gilad Japhet, converts images (face) to short realistic videos. There is only the basic movement of the face, eyes, and mouth. This app has given such life-like results that it is hard to believe that it is a never-existing video created from an image. This software has been used on statutes by archaeologists to see it in action. The most trending in India is the DF of freedom fighter Bhagat Singh. This animation is based on the pre-set driver videos dataset, from which the software chooses the best fit possible. Thus, the animation is slightly different for every image that is converted to video.

| Application/Software/ Program by Company/ Study | Use case | Technique | Website, if any |
|---|---|---|---|
| Deep Nostalgia by MyHeritage | Reviving memories and moments | Image animation using pre-set driving video | www.myheritage.com/ deep-nostalgia |
| Marvel.ai by Veritone | Voice as a Service (VaaS) | Synthetic voice generation | www.veritone.com/ applications/marvelai |
| TrueSync by Flawless | Audio dubbing, lip-sync videos | Audio Synthesis | www.flawlessai.com/ product |

### 7.2.5 INDUSTRY: EDUCATION

If a picture is worth a thousand words, what about a video? What if we can see and hear the characters/famous personalities we read about in our books live!

### 7.2.5.1 Case 10

A DF video was created by a 20th-century renowned artist Salvador Dali in an exhibition in the USA called Dali Lives in an alliance with an ad agency called Goodby, Silverstein & Partners (GS&P). The DF spoke in his voice and accent, curated with hours of research, findings, and hard work [28,29]. Toward the end, Salvador turns around to take a selfie with viewers. As described by its viewers, it was a surreal experience. The voice in the audiobooks can be manipulated according to gender, age, language, and accent, especially for those who understand their native language [30]. Thus, language won't be a barrier to learning.

| Application/Software/ Program of study | Use case | Technique | Website, if any |
|---|---|---|---|
| Dali Lives Exhibition by The Dali and GS&P [14,15] | DF of Salvador Dali | Image animation | https://thedali.org/exhibit/dali-lives/ |

## 7.3 SUMMARY

We discussed a plethora of prospects of DFs in various industries. Also, it doesn't necessarily require an experienced software engineer to create DFs. It is made following the paradigm shift of low code/no code. Nevertheless, its implementation lies in overcoming the existing limitations. The primary obstacles require a massive dataset with high-resolution images and solid graphic cards. Even though there has been research on creating DFs with a few photos, the model was first trained and then utilized on a small dataset. If the industries can capitalize on this technique, it would bring a wave of change for how each sector will work soon.

## REFERENCES

[1] DFs for the Good: A Beneficial Application of Contentious AI Technology, January 2021. doi:10.1007/978-3-030-51328-3_33
[2] Godulla I., Hoffmann C., and Seibert D. (2021) Dealing with DFs – An interdisciplinary examination of the state of research and implications for communication studies in SCM studies. Communication and Media, 10(1),72–96. doi:10.5771/2192-4007-2021-1-72, ISSN online: 2192-4007.
[3] Zhu, B., Fang, H., Sui, Y., and Li, L. (2020). DFs for Medical Video De-Identification: Privacy Protection and Diagnostic Information Preservation. Proceedings of the AAAI/ACM Conference on AI, Ethics, and Society, 414–420. https://doi.org/10.1145/3375627.3375849
[4] Choi, E., Biswal, S. , Malin, B. , Duke, J. , Stewart, W., and Sun, J. (2017). Generating Multi-label Discrete Patient Records Using GANs. In Machine Learning for Healthcare Conference, 286–305. PMLR.
[5] Zhao, H., Li, H., Maurer-Stroh, S., and Cheng, L. (2018). Synthesizing retinal and neuronal images with generative adversarial nets. Medical Image Analysis, 49, 14–26. doi:10.1016/j.media.2018.07.001
[6] Chen, R. J., Lu, M. Y., Chen, T. Y., Williamson, D. F., and Mahmood, F. (2021). Synthetic data in ML for medicine and healthcare. Nature Biomedical Engineering, 5(6), 493–497. https://doi.org/10.1038/s41551-021-00751-8
[7] Joyce, K. E. (2020, October 6). Synthetic data in healthcare advances patient analytics. Search Data Management. https://searchdatamanagement.techtarget.com/feature/Synthetic-data-in-healthcare-advances-patient-analytics
[8] Coffey, K. R., Marx, R. G., and Neumaier, J. F. (2019). DeepSqueak: A deep learning-based system for detection and analysis of ultrasonic vocalizations. Neuropsychopharmacology, 44, 859–868. https://doi.org/10.1038/s41386-018-0303-6
[9] Gaur, L., Afaq, A., Solanki, A., Singh, G., Sharma, S., Jhanjhi, N. Z., … Le, D. (2021). Capitalizing on big data and revolutionary 5G technology: Extracting and visualizing ratings and reviews of global chain hotels. Computers and Electrical Engineering, 95, 107374, ISSN 0045-7906. doi:10.1016/j.compeleceng.2021.107374

[10] Gaur, L., Bhatia, U., Jhanjhi, N. Z., Muhammad, G., and Masud, M. (2021). Medical image-based detection of COVID-19 using deep convolution neural networks. Multimedia Systems, 1–10. doi:10.1007/s00530-021-00794-6

[11] Press Release Rolls Royce Technology breakthrough offers hope for people silenced by disability. Rolls. (n.d.). www.rolls-royce.com/media/press-releases/2019/18-12-2019-technology-breakthrough-offers-hope-for-people-silenced-by-disability.aspx

[12] CB Insights. (2021, June 29). Should brands and retailers adopt synthetic media – The AI for digital content? CB Insights Research. www.cbinsights.com/research/what-is-synthetic-media/

[13] Anshu, K., Gaur, L., and Khazanchi, D. (2017). "Evaluating satisfaction level of grocery E-retailers using intuitionistic fuzzy TOPSIS and ECCSI model," *International Conference on Infocom Technologies and Unmanned Systems (Trends and Future Directions) (ICTUS)*, pp. 276–284. doi:10.1109/ICTUS.2017.8286019

[14] Gaur, L., and Anshu, K. (2018). Consumer preference analysis for websites using e-TailQ and AHP. International Journal of Engineering & Technology, 7(2.11), 14–20.

[15] Gaur L., Agarwal V., and Anshu, K. (2020). "Fuzzy DEMATEL Approach to Identify the Factors Influencing Efficiency of Indian Retail," Strategic System Assurance and Business Analytics. Asset Analytics (Performance and Safety Management). Springer, Singapore. https://doi.org/10.1007/978-981-15-3647-2_

[16] Grey, C. (2020, August 25). Add to Cart: Why DFs Are Good for Retail. AdNews. www.adnews.com.au/news/add-to-cart-why-DFs-are-good-for-retail

[17] Sahu, G., Gaur, L., and Singh, G. (2021). Applying niche and gratification theory approach to examine the users' indulgence towards over-the-top platforms and conventional TV. Telematics and Informatics, 65, 101713. doi:10.1016/j.tele.2021.101713

[18] Ramakrishnan, R., Gaur, L., and Singh, G. (2016). Feasibility and efficacy of BLE beacon IoT devices in inventory management at the shop floor. International Journal of Electrical and Computer Engineering, 6(5), 2362–2368. doi:10.11591/ijece.v6i5.10807

[19] Afaq, A., Gaur, L., Singh, G., and Dhir, A. (2021). COVID-19: Transforming air passengers' behaviour and reshaping their expectations towards the airline industry. Tourism Recreation Research, 1–9. doi:10.1080/02508281.2021.2008211

[20] Gaur, L., Singh, G., Solanki, A., Jhanjhi, N. Z., Bhatia, U., Sharma, S., ... and Kim, W. (2021). Disposition of youth in predicting sustainable development goals using the neuro-fuzzy and random forest algorithms. Human-Centric Computing and Information Sciences, 11, NA.

[21] Singh, G., Kumar, B., Gaur, L., and Tyagi, A. (2019). "Comparison between Multinomial and Bernoulli Naïve Bayes for Text Classification," *2019 International Conference on Automation, Computational and Technology Management (ICACTM)*, pp. 593–596. doi:10.1109/ICACTM.2019.8776800

[22] Gaur, L., Afaq, A., Singh, G., and Dwivedi, Y.K. (2021). Role of artificial intelligence and robotics to foster the touchless travel during a pandemic: A review and research agenda. International Journal of Contemporary Hospitality Management, 33(11), 4079–4098. https://doi.org/10.1108/IJCHM-11-2020-1246

[23] Sharma, S., Singh, G., Gaur, L., and Sharma, R. (2022). Does psychological distance and religiosity influence fraudulent customer behaviour? International Journal of Consumer Studies. doi:10.1111/ijcs.12773

[24] Dietmar, J. (2019, May 21). Council post: GANs and DFs could revolutionize the fashion industry. Forbes. www.forbes.com/sites/forbestechcouncil/2019/05/21/gans-and-DFs-could-revolutionize-the-fashion-industry/?sh=4f638513d17f

[25] Debusmann Jr, B. (2021, March 8). "DF Is the Future of Content Creation." BBC News. www.bbc.com/news/business-56278411

[26] Sharma, D. K., Gaur, L., and Okunbor, D. (2007). Image compression and feature extraction with neural network. Proceedings of the Academy of Information and Management Sciences, 11(1), 33–38.

[27] Rana, J., Gaur, L., Singh, G., Awan, U., and Rasheed, M.I. (2021). Reinforcing customer journey through artificial intelligence: A review and research agenda. International Journal of Emerging Markets, Vol. ahead-of-print (No. ahead-of-print). https://doi.org/10.1108/IJOEM-08-2021-1214

[28] Lee, D. (2019, May 10). DF Salvador Dalí takes selfies with museum visitors. The Verge. www.theverge.com/2019/5/10/18540953/salvador-dali-lives-DF-museum

[29] Westerlund, M. (2019). The emergence of DF technology: A review. Technology Innovation Management Review, 9(11), 39–52. https://doi.org/10.22215/timrev iew/1282

[30] Silbey, J., and Hartzog, W. (2018). The Upside of Deep Fakes. 78 Md. L. Rev. 960 (2019).

# 8 Threats and Challenges by DeepFake Technology

*Mamta Sareen*

## CONTENTS

## 8.1 INTRODUCTION

Recent advances in AI technologies and DL have made substantial steps in image recognition. These technologies, with their potential to generate image datasets, enhance image resolutions, have more extraordinary video predictions and realistic photographs, and have brought about a substantial shift in the field of image processing. One such technology is DeepFake (DF) technology that uses a General Adversarial Network (GAN) where two deep neural networks are trained to work in tandem. These networks iteratively go back and forth between the genuine/sample image and the statistically generated image until their differences are minimal. This method showed the likelihood of developing fake photos or creating fake ones by replacing people's faces with other ones. This technology gave a revolutionized approach to creating morphed videos much faster. One genius example of DF technology is of a reputed soccer player, David Beckham, who speaks nine languages fluently [1]. The initial intent of creating such videos was harmless and aimed at providing a research tool of artificial video generation that can be useful for movies, storytelling, and other modern-day multimedia services.

DOI: 10.1201/9781003231493-8

This technology, though, available was still ubiquitous until the mid-2010s. However, a composite video of former US president Barrack Obama released in 2017, which showed him speaking words from an alternative soundtrack, became viral and paved a path to the explosive growth of DFs in current times [2]. The technology had blossomed like some poisonous flower and was everywhere, even available to amateurs. It provided them the opportunity to be mischievous. A typical example is a fake video showing former US President Barack Obama making some out-of-character statements that got 5 million views and 83,000 plus shares on Facebook and other social media platforms [3,4,5]. However, this video was a fake video using AI which synthesized US actor-comedian Jordan Peele's face impersonating Obama with his voice.

Another example is a video involving US President Donald Trump, where he is making a challenging statement so that Belgium is provoked to withdraw from the Paris agreement. A Belgian political party published the video on Twitter and Facebook but was eventually exposed by Lead Stories [6]. The creator intended to grab people's attention and redirect them toward an online petition. This small-scale demonstration was enough to raise concerns on how DFs can threaten the already-vulnerable global systems. The DFs, along with their extensive spread through social media platforms, have raised substantial concerns worldwide regarding the credibility of digital media. The constant news about the impact made by these DF videos on both individuals and organizations has presented various security challenges. This paper is a modest attempt to point out multiple threats and challenges posed by DF technology.

## 8.2   DFS AND THEIR GROWTH

In 1990, Graber, through his landmark experiment, proved the impact of visual communication as vast and influential [7]. Grabe and Bucy in 2009 [8] and Prior in 2013 [9] further substantiated their idea of visual communication, which demonstrated higher levels of recall and impact of users who were given visual aids. These studies proved that visuals cause a stronger reaction than words and help users engage with content, thereby influencing information retention. People find images and audio-visual content more accessible to understand than written text as this gives them a "metacognitive experience" [10]. In today's world, information plays a significant role, and people generally do not have time and energy to check the authenticity of the information they acquire. So direct visual perception is usually assumed to be trustworthy. Through these visuals, the general public or consumers acquire specific knowledge that helps them make significant decisions about people, institutions, organizations, and even leaders. Consumers of these videos are found to accept video evidence more profoundly than other sources of information. Thus, videos prove beneficial when collective agreement on a topic is required [11].

DF technology uses this authority of visual communication to create a form of visual disinformation by influencing the sentiments and perceptions of people. A well-timed fake video of an influential leader talking about racism or terrorism has the potential to send shock waves through the world media. Certain factors tend to fuel the DF fire. Some of them can be stated as follows:

**Information cascade:** David et al. described information cascade as the base of viral content. It results when people don't believe their information but rely more on the authentication of others' information and then pass it along further [12]. Social media platforms provide the right environment for the information cascades to spread its content and spill it over to mass audience. Black Lives Matter activists or the Never Again movement of the Parkland High School students are just a few examples of information cascade [13,14]. According to the study, hoaxes and fake rumors can reach people ten times faster than real stories [15]. It has been proved that the retentivity of negative information is more than positive information [15]. Aided with human's natural penchant toward certain stimuli such as porn, gossip, and violence, DFs provide just "the right environment" to fuel this tendency. Individuals maliciously playing with DFs can quickly reach a massive, even global audience.

**Timing of circulation:** Perilous time is the basic idea behind the creation of DFs. Certain moments, in any event, are crucial or sensitive and might tilt the outcome of the event in any direction. Suppose any fake video showing some immediately unverifiable facts is circulated among the users at a sensitive time. In that case, the chances are that it could leave an immediate and immense impact on the minds of the recipients and can be instrumental in changing their opinion regarding the fact shown. The distribution of fake videos is set to be so narrow that by the time the video is debunked, an irrevocable impact is already made. These intentionally distorted videos circulated through social media can cloud reality at a time. For example, time just before the voting day in any election is very crucial. Suppose any fake video showing a candidate's corrupt behavior (which he did not do) is circulated among voters before being publicly verified. In that case, it might prejudice voters' minds and might have a consequential impact on the results of elections.

**Speed of circulation:** Gone are the times when the ability of an individual or an organization to distribute images information in the form of audio or video is limited. The information revolution has drastically changed the content distribution model. Today, many online platforms facilitate global connectivity, thereby democratizing access to information to an unparalleled degree. The content to be distributed can find its way to many international audiences. The speed at which the fake video is circulated online sets the platform of its effectiveness.

**Digital literacy:** Some researchers believe that those developing countries where the penetration of digital literacy is relatively low are more vulnerable to fall prey to disinformation caused by DFs. The consumers of media in these countries are not well versed with the techniques of differentiating the real from the fake, and the probability of them accepting the artificial as truth is high. In one such incident, the violence inflicted on the Rohingya community in Myanmar was due to falsified posts that propagated on Facebook [16]. DFs could similarly be used as a tool of subjugation by authoritarian regimes or extremist groups to invoke social division.

In 2021, the Federal Bureau of Investigation (FBI) issued a warning regarding the fake media content as a newly defined cyberattack causing considerable financial and reputational impacts to organizations and society in general [17]. Understanding the underlying threats posed by DFs is essential to formulate any countermeasures to combat them.

## 8.3   THREAT OF DFS

The main motive of the creator of a DF is to spread disinformation and make consumers believe in what has been shown to them. The movie industry uses this technology for special effects and animations that seem harmless. However, this technology is now being used for nefarious purposes by tech-savvy criminals. The DF technology appears to have introduced a new class of media that malicious users are using to their advantage. DFs can threaten political elections, cybersecurity, individual and corporate finances, reputations, and much more, among the potential risks. Below are a few of the possible threats posed by DF technology.

## 8.4   THREATS TO NATIONAL SECURITY

DFs can significantly pose threats to any national security if maliciously deployed by the hands of bad actors. Many researchers, practitioners, and government representatives of various countries are worried about the national security-related implications of DFs. The lawmakers in the US are expressing their concerns about the disinformation campaigns in the US elections that have the potential to aggravate political and social divisions in the society and pose a threat to national security [18]. According to the Director of the Pentagon's Joint AICenter, "DFs is a national security issue" [19]. Also, the Director of National Intelligence, Daniel R. Coats, quoted that "Adversaries and strategic competitors probably will attempt to use deep fakes or similar machine-learning technologies to create convincing – but false – image, audio, and video files to augment influence campaigns directed against the United States and our allies and partners" [20]. Various commentators, experts, and analysts have also seconded these conclusions.

Wrong information spread through DFs could endanger national security in numerous ways. For example, misinformation could jeopardize the safety of any nation's military forces working with any foreign civilian population if any DF showing military members assaulting or killing civilians is circulated. Any malicious person could take the advantage of a region's instability (which is quite common nowadays) by spreading fake content through DFs to exacerbate the local population, leading to civilian casualties. Hostile foreign regimes could also use DFs to create propaganda, showing world leaders behaving offensively or hostilely. For example, Chesney and Citron, in their paper, posed a scenario of the repercussions of a fake video of an American general in Afghanistan burning a Koran. Currently, we are living in a world already primed for violence; such disinformation could become a powerful tool for potential incitement [21]. These are just a few of the instances stated where a highly realistic DF can pose a unique threat to public safety and national security.

## 8.5 THREAT TO INDIVIDUALS

History has witnessed the consequences of lies about what people have done or said. With its inherent credibility and the ability to hide the liar's creative role, DF technology comes as a powerful tool to exploit or sabotage others. Since this technology allows to manipulate an individual's voice, face, and body in the video, it gives limitless opportunities to malicious users to exploit their identity for malicious indulgence. It can provide a significant blow to any individual across any field of competition, whether it be a workplace, sports, politics, romance, or personal life. The right combination of algorithmic boosting, cognitive biases, and ever-improving search engines increases the circulation for such scandalous fakes.

The virtual world is frequently faced with DF sex videos primarily designed for the creator's sexual or financial gratification. A typical example is the attempt to tarnish the dignity of journalist Rana Ayyub by morphing her face onto another woman's body and creating a 2-minute fake pornographic video [22]. This was in retaliation to her article against corruption in Hindu nationalist politics. Such an act imposes direct psychological harm to anyone and sabotages their reputation, thereby inflicting damage in other dimensions. DF videos can be a handy tool for blackmailers to exploit and extract something of value from them. Even if someone has nothing to lose, undoing the initial damage done by DFs could force people to succumb to the threat and provide money, information, and so forth. As seen in the previous example, DF can exploit an individual's sexual identity. It is feared that DF sex videos can force individuals into virtual sex and transmute rape threats into a frightening virtual reality. Alternatively, DF depicting violence or abusive behavior of an individual may be used to threaten, bully, or impose psychological harm on the targeted individual.

Aided with the technological support of ease of copying and storage in remote jurisdictions, eliminating these fakes becomes harder once they are posted and shared. Depending upon the timing, situation, and circulation of DFs videos, the effects could be devastating. It could lead to the loss of unique opportunity or the loss of support of friends or the denial of a promotion or denial in romance or to the cancellation of a business opportunity, and beyond. At times, debunking the authenticity of the fake may come too late to remedy the initial harm.

## 8.6 THREAT TO SOCIETY

DF technology impacts individuals and may have devastating consequences on the society if not controlled in a timely manner. DFs can influence the sentiments and perceptions of people and, if done maliciously, can negatively impact the community. In 2018, a video went viral on Indian social media that purportedly showed a child while playing in Bangalore being abducted by two men [23]. Although this so-called kidnapping demonstrated in the video was not real, it created widespread confusion and panic, resulting in an eight-week period of mob violence that took the lives of at least nine innocent people. Consider the following scenarios and their incredible impact on the society:

- Fake videos featuring public officials involved in unlawful activities such as taking bribes, engaging in adultery, giving hate speeches, etc.
- Fake videos target famous or well-reputed personalities of the society by creating altered pornographic clips.
- Circulating fake videos involving politicians and other government officials in situations or places where they were not and saying or doing evil things that they did not. For example, it could create videos of them collaborating with spies or criminals.
- Fake videos of soldiers murdering innocent people can precipitate waves of violence among people and, in the worst case, can lead to civil disobedience.
- Fake videos displaying brutality against a particular caste or race can augment the already present social divisions and trigger actions or even violence.
- Fake audio or video could provoke the youth to realize a degree of mobilization-to-action that written words alone could not achieve.

DFs can result in people attaining false beliefs, i.e., they might believe these fakes to be genuine. This may have dire practical consequences as DFs not only would cause false premises but also inculcate the habit of undermining justification for true beliefs. As a result, there might be low trust levels of real videos from legitimate news media [21,24]. The presence of such fake videos on social media and other electronic media can dissuade the very basis of any society and impose costs. These costs could either be intangible in maintaining/improving societal divisions or tangible costs for those who have been tricked into certain actions and those who have suffered from those actions.

## 8.7 THREATS TO JUDICIAL SYSTEMS

DF is still an emerging topic in the law. Though DF research dates back to early 2014, the actual impact on the judicial system is now becoming a matter of concern among legal scholars and policymakers. Any judicial system relies heavily on pieces of evidence. One of the major concerns is the threat imposed by DF poses regarding tampering of evidence [25]. This may inadvertently pose problems for courts in accepting the legitimacy of litigants or witnesses. How DFs tamper, the proof can even condemn the innocent or forgive the guilty. It is felt that unforeseen issues may arise during cross-examinations when one party involved testifies favorably concerning the details of a DF video and the other party (opposing) denies its authenticity. This would negatively impact the court cases and impose additional overhead in terms of both time and money in authenticating the produced evidence. One such example is a child custody case in the UK where the mother made a DF audio file of the father showing violent behavior as evidence [26]. Though this evidence was dismissed after its forensic examination, it raises multiple questions on the plausibility of an erroneous judgment.

DFs can also cause additional caseload in the courts with the overhead of cases where a DF video gives rise to a misdemeanor claim. They may also affect the courts by playing a subsidiary role in disputes they did not cause by adding just another piece of evidence in litigation and biasing the judgment process. Fake videos might accidentally or maliciously end up archiving historically considered trustworthy, such as those of media news. Suppose the custodian of those media records does not timely detect DF. In that case, there is a risk that the custodian might unintentionally vouch for a DF when called upon to authenticate evidence in a court proceeding. Further, since DFs are so common, the overhead procedure of verifying the authenticity of the actual evidence might sow doubt in the jury/judge's mind. Thus, if the jury/judge who is entrusted with the crucial role of the truth of fact starts to doubt and be skeptical, then the very basis of the justice system might shake.

## 8.8 THREATS TO POLITICS OR DEMOCRATIC DISCOURSE

Any democracy relies majorly on online propaganda as it is the cheapest tool to wield a high degree of influence. DFs are quick to create and easy to circulate to a broad audience and hence can deliberately or unknowingly be used to misinform the public for political advantage. Because it is harder for an ordinary person to differentiate between a real and a DF video, these fakes can alter the very sense of the reality of the video. An altered video of an American politician, Nancy Pelosi, became viral on social media, showing her mispronouncing her words under intoxication. When shared by the then US President Donald J. Trump, this fake got more than 2.5 million shares on Facebook only [27]. Such fakes can alter public perception, and by the time they are proven to be counterfeit, the damage seems to have already been done. A recent imitation of Joe Biden showing him not knowing which state he is in receives 1 million views on Twitter [28].

DF technology can sow unprecedented amounts of disinformation and lower the voter's level of faith in democracy [29]. DFs attack the very basis of democracy and can be termed as inherently antidemocratic. Though illusory images are often used to disrepute political opponents, DFs offer a more convincing illusion than single images. It is not difficult for a well-funded government propaganda agency to create humiliating DFs of individuals who pose political hurdles. Such fakes might create difficulties for opposition movements.

Further, public discourse is often used to get an insight of people on various policy matters. Sometimes lies spread by DFs have intentions to challenge the integrity and reliability of participants in such debates. At other times, these lies are so potent that they can erode the factual foundation of policy discourse. DFs could provide "evidence" to people looking to further their cognitive dissonance around disinformation. Democratic discourse works at its best when discussions/debates are based on shared truths and facts backed by empirical evidence. In the absence of such verifying facts, efforts to solve major national issues remain entangled in needless first-order questions. DFs have caused a large-scale erosion of public faith in presented facts and statistics and can cause difficulties in democratic discourse proceedings. It is hard for truthful facts to emerge from the scrum of flooded DFs.

## 8.9 THREAT TO ELECTIONS

Elections are times of high risk, and a realistic DF can potentially impact voters immediately. A well-timed DF can interfere in the state or central elections by circulating substantial fiction and ambiguity regarding the candidates' personal life and policy positions into the electoral process. Such uncertainty has the potential to destabilize the consequence of any election. These DFs are timed in a specific period, allowing enough time for its circulation but not enough time frame to debunk it effectively. This limited period has the potential to cloud reality and tilt the outcome of any election in anyone's favor. A UK-based study found that DFs tend to confuse people regarding the real or fake information circulating on the internet, and consequently, they tend to trust less in the news on social media [30].

Further, the fewer people trust news media, the more probable they are to fall for disinformation floating on social or electronic media, which in turn can impact their voting behavior [31]. It can be pretty impactful if DFs are combined with political microtargeting techniques. Few scenarios where DF can influence elections could be:

- A DF impersonates a news anchor in providing false voting information, thereby creating confusion on the election day.
- Malicious political actors can use DFs to forge evidence to fuel their counterparts' false allegations and fake narratives.
- A DF imitating a candidate and showing them saying certain words can drastically impact the candidate's reputation.
- DFs can come in handy in creating new fictitious content of controversial or hateful statements to incite political divisions or even violence.
- A DF video shows candidates in challenging situations or with people, which may create distrust.
- Conversely, candidates or various political actors/stakeholders can doubt factual information harmful to their reputation by calling it a DF.
- Political actors might use DF as a hypothetical threat to make unsubstantial claims and confuse voters—for example, the 2020 Georgian parliamentary elections incident.

In a study in Singapore, although 54% of respondents were conscious of the perception of DFs, one in three of those respondents still shared the content of such DFs on social media [32]. If there is a large-scale promotion of such DFs, it might prove to be successful in influencing people. A voter who is misinformed/disinformed is unable to judiciously cast a vote and thus indirectly deprive voters of their right to vote that, in a real sense, is based on accurate knowledge of politicians' stances [29]. Also, in situations of political polarization, people tend to believe more in such "information" that approves their viewpoints. Thus, the chances of becoming more susceptible to being influenced by misinformation increase dramatically. DFs can influence the outcome of any election, especially if the timing chosen for the distribution of such manipulated media is enough for circulation but less time left for the victim to debunk it effectively.

## 8.10   THREATS TO BUSINESSES

DFs pose a significant threat to businesses in this age where virtual interactions and digital media is the standard form of communication adopted by most organizations. No longer is the DF technology used for pornographic-related content, but it has now maliciously moved to target organizations by releasing misinformation and disinformation. Many publicly available examples depict criminals using visual and audio DFs for committing frauds or crimes, including blackmail, identity theft, and social engineering. One can imagine the impact on the organization's reputations or irrevocable damage to the trust of shareholders when one sees a DF showing a CEO of a company confessing financial fraud or accepting a bribe. Some of the scenarios that have the potential to harm businesses can be:

- **Phishing scams:** DFs can be used to synthetically impersonate a colleague or a client to divulge sensitive information or details on any project or give access to the company's database.
- **Transaction scams:** There are many instances where scam creators have targeted company employees and convinced them through audio or video DF to make certain payments. Among various examples, one such example is of a UK-based energy firm making a transfer of $243,000 after being duped by a DF.
- **Extortion scam:** DFs as a blackmail tool to extort money from a company by threatening to release a DF video with compromising content.

The above are just a few instances stated that may pose a severe threat to the reputation of any business. Already organizations are dealing with various social engineering attacks, and the additional burden of combating DFs can have an adverse budgetary impact on businesses. According to the findings of Forrester Research, a monetary loss of $250 million was predicted to occur by the end of 2020 from DF technology.

## 8.11 THE THREAT IN CORRODING TRUST IN INSTITUTIONS

Public institutions, such as judges, juries, elected officials, legislators, appointed officials, etc., form the foundation of the society. The public trusts these institutions and the people associated with them. If any institution plays a significant role in any organization, it is a potential target for DF technology. A fake and viral video showing a judge abusing his authority or a high police official involved in a crime or a member of parliament speaking the racist language are fuel enough to erode the public's trust in such institutions and, at times, the very foundation of any society. Already such institutions or people associated with them are subject to reputational attacks, and the DF technology further makes it harder to deflate/debunk such claims. In 2020, a conservative political activist Theodora Dickinson shared a video with her tweet demanding, "In response to the New Zealand Mosque attacks, Islamists have burned down a Christian church in Pakistan. Why is this not being shown on @BBCNews?!" [33]. However, the video was fake and belonged to an attack on the church in Egypt in 2013. Such disinformation/misinformation can instigate racism or insecurity among the general public, especially if trusted people of society share them. Fake and provocative videos easily find a primed audience, especially where there is already a presence of solid narratives of distrust either in policies or political leaders or societal regulations or religious faith or any forthcoming law. We live in a society whose foundations are already very fragile, and any such incidents of distrust can prove to be quite fatal.

## 8.12   COUNTERMEASURES

The potential for nefarious use of DF technology to perpetrate damage and inflict harm to the society, the election system, individuals, and institutions has raised alarms to seek effective countermeasures to combat them. Studies into the impact of DFs and ways to mitigate against the risks they pose have identified the following critical areas of countermeasures.

## 8.13   LEGISLATIVE MEASURES

Currently, most countries are not legally prepared to deal with DFs. There is no law or civil liability regime in most nations against the creation or distribution of DFs. Countries need to accept DFs as a potential threat and make laws that criminally prosecute those who transgress the laid down versions of the truth. Mere banning DFs is not desirable as digital manipulation has inherently benefitted too. What is needed is crafting a law that prohibits the destructive applications of DF technology and simultaneously excludes the beneficial ones. The mere existence of a law banning DFs be enough to cast a significant shadow and act as a deterrent to its usage.

The awareness in this direction has started, and legislators in various countries are working to develop new laws for disinformation. Lawmakers of New York are working on the bill that forbids the specific usage of a "digital replica" of a person [34]. US legislation is stated to develop a bill that establishes criminal penalties for anyone found guilty of usage/production of DFs and insists the producers of DFs abide by specific verifying techniques such as the digital watermark to ensure the authentication of the media [35]. Singapore recently passed legislation that empowers the government to order social media platforms to remove any content that it considers to be false [36]. However, such legislations have their aftereffects. They need thorough research on possible misuse as chances are there that, if misused, they could also be used to suppress free speech under the umbrella of tackling disinformation. The government must encourage social media platforms to be more vigilant, pay closer attention to the content being posted on their platforms, and pass laws/regulations. Further, there is a need to review the non-consensual sharing of sexual images to restrict DF pornography. Laws should be made to criminalize the making or sharing of DFs with malicious intent. However, legal remedies are generally applied ex post facto and will thus have a limited impact in addressing the possible scale of the damage.

## 8.14   TECHNOLOGICAL COUNTERMEASURES

There exist specific technical solutions as possible countermeasures against DFs. DF is the product of AI, and technology only can come to counteract the threats posed by them. While technology is the initiator of the problem, technology also offers a potential solution to combat their growing threat. The technical countermeasures can be broadly categorized as:

**Detection:** One such containment tool uses multi-modal detection techniques to find any tampering in the target media. The following are some of the technical solutions available commercially:

- **Video Authenticator Tool:** Launched by Microsoft in 2020, it detects the amalgamation boundary of the DF and understated grayscale elements and even provides a confidence score of the manipulation.
- **Biological Signals**: A tool developed by the researchers from Binghamton University and Intel looks for unique natural and generative noise signals left by DF model videos and can obtain around 97.29% accuracy for fake video detection.
- **Phoneme-Viseme Mismatches:** Researchers from Stanford University and the University of California developed another tool that matches visemes, the dynamics of the mouth shape with phoneme, the spoken words to detect even spatially small and temporally localized manipulations in DF videos.
- **Recurrent Convolutional Models (RCMs):** This technique uses temporal information from image streams across domains and detects face manipulation in videos. In video streams, it can detect DF, Face2Face, and FaceSwap tampered faces.

The above-stated techniques try to detect certain inconsistencies generated by DFs that are hard for humans to notice using ML and AI. Hence, if readily accessible tools flood the market to create fake videos, technology also gives equally accessible tools to detect them. It is always merely a tug-of-war between both the bad and good "actors" of technology.

**Media authentication:** It is one such tool that can authenticate the origin and content of the media creator. This authentication could be achieved using a watermarking chain of custody logging or other available means. This will allow users to see if the media has been tampered with or manipulated and thus put retardation on fake video generation. Various tools such as FotoForensics, Jeffrey's Exif Viewer, TinEye, etc. are available in the market that aid the forensics of any media.

**Media provenance:** Adding provenance information and attaching it to the media helps make trustworthy content easier to identify. The provenance information consists of basic information on media starting from the origin of media to other sites of its publication. Any single fake image can easily be detected using reverse image search on the internet. If the DF used another embodiment somewhere on the internet for its creation, the original image would appear in the search. Some of the media provenance solutions that are available on the internet today can be listed as follows:

- *YouTube Content ID:* YouTube provides a Content ID to the copyright owners to identify and manage their content. This ID is monitored by YouTube for any matches with an already existent database to check for any violation of copyright.
- *Adobe Content Authenticity Initiative:* Adobe provides provenance by giving creators an option to claim authorship and authorizing consumers to evaluate the trustworthiness of the content.
- *Microsoft Aether Media Provenance (AMP):* Microsoft AMP allows the users to create signed manifests for the created media that can also be registered and signed by chain-of-custody ledgers like blockchain. If the required AMP

manifest is successfully located, it is communicated to the consumer via visual elements in the browser.

- *FuJo Provenance:* An EU project named PROVENANCE was initiated in 2018 to develop an intermediary-free solution for digital content verification. The PROVENANCE verification layer is intended to use advanced tools such as semantic uplift, image forensics, and cascade analysis to detect any alterations to the media content.

**Monitoring**: The effectiveness of all of the above-stated countermeasures would be enhanced if it is clubbed with societal awareness. DFs are more of a societal issue than a technological one as they are more prevalent in polarization places. Organizations need to reframe their security policies and add multiple checkpoints to possible situations where DFs might cause problems. Conducting crisis management exercises might limit the successful DF attempts. Individuals most at risk, such as celebrities or senior executives of large companies, need to follow specific measures to counterbalance the dangers posed by a DF attack. Web monitoring is the best measure to identify and combat the spread of DFs at the earliest stage.

**Enhancing media literacy:** Media literacy is yet another effective tool to combat disinformation caused by DFs. Improving media literacy to cultivate a discerning public is one of the precursors to combat the challenges posed by DFs. As consumers of media, people need to develop the ability to decipher, understand, and differentiate between fake and reality. People need to pause before blindly believing in what they are seeing. And this could be achieved by effective media awareness among consumers. The cheaply made DFs leave certain artifacts that can help detect the manipulation when observed keenly. There are specific telltale characteristics of a cheap DF video that, if keenly observed, can help identify them. For example, a manipulated video will have skin that appears too smooth or too wrinkly, shadows near eyes and eyebrows are often incongruent, mismatch of the agedness of the skin and that of the hair and eyes, unnatural eye movement, strange facial expressions, body shape or hair, abnormal skin colors, inconsistent head positions, etc.; these are some pointers that, if made aware to the public, can restrict the viral distribution of the fake videos.

The above-stated measures are some of the ways one can contain if not fully combat the impact made by the DFs; however, doubts persist about the effectiveness of different interpositions. As DFs are born through adversarial training, there is a high probability that these DF's ability to evade AI-based detection methods might improve as they get more familiarized with such detection techniques. There seems to be a "cat-and-mouse" process prejudiced in favor of the mice, especially in the long term. Most DF detection countermeasures are concentrated on achieving short-term solutions, with an expectation that legislative or monitoring techniques might prove more beneficial as a long-term solution to the threat posed by DFs. This chapter highlights some of the dangers and possible consequences of DF technology. However, there is a dire need for policymakers, researchers, and consumers to scan the horizon for new technological and non-technical innovations that can act as a deterrent to the growing threat levels of visual disinformation created by DFs. Continuous exploration of piloting new containment measures is needed at a pace that matches the speed at which the DF technology is progressing. Further, it is high time that consumers do not believe entirely in what they see or hear and rather exercise their wisdom to confirm its trustworthiness.

## 8.15 SUMMARY

Suppose every video has the potential to be fake. In that case, it offers people the opportunity to challenge the integrity of genuine footage, leading to the breakdown of people's beliefs. It is stated that DF technology is slowly leading people toward an "infopocalypse" where it is difficult to differentiate between fake and real [37]. It could lead to a situation where commonly held reality and beliefs fall apart and chaos reigns. Human beings are generally [38,39,40] attracted more to negative and novel information. There is a dire need for collaborative actions across legislative regulations, platform policies, technology intervention, and media literacy that can provide countermeasures to mitigate the threat of malicious DFs.

## REFERENCES

[1] Malaria Must Die. (2019, April 9). David Beckham speaks nine languages to launch Malaria Must Die Voice Petition. YouTube. Retrieved June 9, 2021, from www.yout ube.com/watch?v= QiiSAvKJIHo

[2] BuzzFeed/YouTube. (2018, April 17). You won't believe what Obama says in this video!

[3] YouTube. (2018, April 17). You won't believe what Obama says in this video! www. youtube.com/watch?v=cQ54GDm1eL0 and www.youtube.com/watch?v=cQ54GD (video unavailable at present).

[4] Twitter. (2018, April 17). You won't believe what Obama says in this video! https:// twitter.com/BuzzFeed/status/9862579917 99222272

[5] Facebook. (2018, April 17). You won't believe what Obama says in this video! www. facebook.com/watch/?v=10157675 129905329

[6] Lytvynenko, J. (2018). "A Belgian Political Party Is Circulating a Trump DF Video," BuzzFeed News, 20 May 2018. [Online]. Available: www.buzzfeednews.com/article/ janelytvynenko/a-belgian-political-party-just-published-a-DF-video

[7] Graber, D. A. (1990). Seeing is remembering: How visuals contribute to learning from television news. Journal of Communication, 40(3), 134–156.

[8] Grabe, M. E., & Bucy, E. P. (2009). *Image Bite Politics: News and the Visual Framing of Elections*. Oxford University Press.

[9] Prior, M. (2013). Visual political knowledge: A different road to competence? Journal of Politics, 76(1), 41–57.

[10] Schwarz, N., Sanna, L. J., Skurnik, I., & Yoon, C. (2007). Metacognitive experiences and the intricacies of setting people straight: Implications for debiasing and public information campaigns. Advances in Experimental Social Psychology, 39, 127–161.

[11] Rini, R. (2019). DFs and the epistemic backstop. https://philpapers.org/rec/RINDAT

[12] David Easley & Jon Kleinberg, Networks, Crowds, And Markets: Reasoning About A Highly Connected World. (2010). (Exploring Cognitive Biases in the Information Marketplace); Cass Sunstein, Republic.Com 2.0 (2007).

[13] Anderson, M., & Hitlin, P., The Hashtag #BlackLivesMatter Emerges: Social Activism on Twitter, PEW RES. CTR. (Aug. 15, 2016), www.pewInternet.org/2016/08/15/the hashtag-blacklivesmatter-emerges-social-ctivism-on-twitter

[14] Bromwich, J. E. (Mar. 7, 2018). How the Parkland Students Got So Good at Social Media, The New York Times, www.nytimes.com/2018/03/07/us/parkland-students-social-media.html [https://perma.cc/7AW9-4HR2

[15] Vosoughi, S. et al., The Spread of True and False News Online, 359 SCIENCE 1146, (2018), http://science.sciencemag.org/content/359/6380/1146/tab-pdf [https://perma.cc/5U5DUHPZ

[16] www.nytimes.com/2018/11/06/technology/myanmar-facebook.html

[17] www.wilmerhale.com/en/insights/client-alerts/20200316-fbi-warns-companies-of-almost-certain-threats-from-DFs

[18] https://schiff.house.gov/imo/media/doc/2018-09%20ODNI%20Deep%20Fakes%20letter.pdf

[19] US House of Representatives, Hearing on National Security Challenges of AI, Manipulated Media and DFs, 13/VI/2019.

[20] Worldwide Threat Assessment of the US Intelligence Community, Statement for the Record, 29/I/2019, p. 7.

[21] Chesney, R., & Citron, D. K. (2019). DFs and the new information war. Foreign Affairs, January/February, 147–155.

[22] Rana Ayyub, In India, Journalists Face Slut-Shaming and Rape Threats, The New York Times (May 22, 2018), www.nytimes.com/2018/05/22/opinion/india-journalists-slut-shamingrape.html; [https://perma.cc/A7WR-PF6L]; 'I Couldn't Talk or Sleep for Three Days': Journalist Rana Ayyub's Horrific Social Media Ordeal over Fake Tweet, Daily O (Apr. 26, 2018), www.dailyo.in/variety/rana-ayyub-trolling-fake-tweet-social-media-harassmenthindutva/story/1/23733.html

[23] www.bbc.com/news/world-asia-india-44435127

[24] Toews, R. (2020). DFs are going to wreak havoc on society. We are not prepared. Forbes. www.forb es.com/sites/robtoews/2020/05/25/DFs-are-going-to-wreak-havoc-on-society-weare-not-prepared/

[25] Pfefferkorn, R. (2020). "'DFs' in the courtroom," Boston University Law Journal, 29(2), 245–276.

[26] Ryan, P. 'DF' Audio Evidence Used in UK Court to Discredit Dubai Dad, THE NATIONAL (Feb. 8, 2020), www.thenational.ae/uae/courts/DF-audio-evidenceused-in-uk-court-to-discredit-dubai-dad-1.975764

[27] Owen, L. H. What Do We Do About the "Shallowfake" Nancy Pelosi Video and Others Like It?, NIEMAN LAB (May 31, 2019), www.niemanlab.org/2019/05/whatdo-we-do-about-the-shallowfake-nancy-pelosi-video-and-others-like-it/

[28] Kelly, M. (2019). "Distorted Nancy Pelosi videos show platforms aren't ready to fight dirty campaign tricks." [Online]. Available: www.theverge.com/2019/5/24/18637771/nancy-pelosi-congress-DF-video-facebook-twitter-youtube

[29] Green, R. (2019). Counterfeit Campaign Speech. Hastings Law Journal, 70(6), 1445–1490.

[30] Vaccari, C., & Chadwick, A. (2020). DFs and disinformation: Exploring the impact of synthetic political video on deception, uncertainty, and trust in news. Social Media + Society, 1–13. https://doi.org/10.1177/2056305120903408

[31] Zimmermann, F., & Kohring, M. (2020). Mistrust, disinforming news, and vote choice: A panel survey on the origins and consequences of believing disinformation in the 2017 German Parliamentary Election. Political Communication, 37, 215–237. doi:10.1080/10584609.2019.1686095

[32] https://sea.mashable.com/tech/13337/think-you-can-spot-a-DF-survey-proves-that-even-the-best-get-fooled

[33] www.theguardian.com/technology/ng-interactive/2019/jun/22/the-rise-of-the-DF-and-the-threat-to-democracy; www.nysenate.gov/legislation/bills/2017/a8155

[34] www.bu.edu/bulawreview/files/2021/04/LANGA.pdf

[35] www.congress.gov/bill/116th-congress/house-bill/3230

[36] www.bbc.com/news/world-asia-48196985

[37] Rothman, J. (2018). In the age of A.I., is seeing still believing? New Yorker. www.newyorker. com/magazine/2018/11/12/in-the-age-of-ai-is-seeing-still-believing

[38] Mahbub, Md. K., Biswas, M., Gaur, L., Alenezi, F., & Santosh, K. (2022). Deep features to detect pulmonary abnormalities in chest X-rays due to infectious disease X: Covid-19, pneumonia, and tuberculosis. Information Sciences, 592, 389–401. https://doi.org/10.1016/J.INS.2022.01.062

[39] Sharma, S., Singh, G., Gaur, L., & Sharma, R. (2022). Does psychological distance and religiosity influence fraudulent customer behavior? International Journal of Consumer Studies. 10.1111/ijcs.12773

[40] Zaman, N., & Gaur, L. (2022). Approaches and Applications of Deep Learning in Virtual Medical Care. IGI. doi:10.4018/978-1-7998-8929-8.ch002

# 9 DeepFakes, Media, and Societal Impacts

*Shubha Mishra, Piyush Kumar Shukla, and Ratish Agrawal*

## CONTENTS

## 9.1 INTRODUCTION

The calculations that construct DeepFakes (DFs) are simpler to construct than identity. Based on the exceptional nature of the Generative Antagonistic Systems utilized agreeing to Goodfellow, these models are built by setting "counterfeiters" against "police," and fruitful models by definition have, as of now, appeared that the fake could beat location strategies. Without a doubt, since DFs have relocated from beat computer science research facilities to cheap program stages worldwide, analysts are moreover centering on careful calculations that might distinguish the misdirection (see Tolosana et al. [1] for a later survey). But Seitz was not certain of this technique and compared the winding of misdirection and location with an arms race [2,3], with the calculations that hoodwink having the early advantage compared with those that identify.

The moment's eye-opener was the numerous social and mental questions that these DFs raised: does presentation to DFs weaken belief within the media? How might DFs be utilized amid social intuition? Are there methodologies for debunking or countering DFs? Still, to date, there have been a modest bunch of social researchers who have inspected the social effect of the innovation. It is time to understand the potential impacts of DFs on individuals and how mental and media speculations apply.

## 9.2 A SHORTAGE OF EXPERIMENTAL INQUIRE ABOUT

At the time of this composing, as it were, a couple of things have inspected the social effect of DFs [4], despite the notoriety of confronting swap stages (e.g., the Zao app [5]). This special issue looked out for the primary era of DF investigation that analyzes the mental, social, and approach suggestions of a world in which individuals

DOI: 10.1201/9781003231493-9

can effortlessly deliver and spread the recordings of occasions that never really happened, but which is unclear from genuine recordings.

Even though there have been a handful of considerations looking at false memory securing and social impact from changed still pictures (i.e., Garry and Swim [3]), the mental forms and results of seeing counterfeit insights (AI)-modified video stay generally unstudied. Shockingly, the leading beginning point for understanding the effect of DFs is immersive virtual reality (VR). In VR, one can construct "doppelgangers," three-dimensional (3D) models of a given individual, based on photogrammetry and other strategies that make a 3D structure from an arrangement of two-dimensional (2D) pictures. Once the doppelganger is built, it is essential to apply stock animations onto the 3D models. After that, the individuals appear in the VR DF scene, either in a head-mounted show or rendered as a typical 2D video activity. VR DFs are impactful.

Compared with observing scenes of another individual, observing your claim doppelganger causes encoding of untrue recollections in which members accept that they performed the DF action, more workout behavior after observing a positive well-being result, and brand inclination for items utilized by the virtual self within the DF [6]. It is profoundly plausible that unused mental components and results are at play when a DF video is perceptually vague from an actual video.

## 9.3   A FEW BITS OF KNOWLEDGE FROM DOUBLE-DEALING INVESTIGATE

Double-dealing at the center of DFs includes intentioned, intentionally, and deliberately deceiving another individual [7]. The misdirection location writing proposes that individuals are not especially great at identifying duplicity when evaluating messages and can quickly obtain false convictions. Meta-analyses of double-dealing location consider recommending that individuals perform as it were marginally over chance when assessing a statement as either genuine or misleading. Imperatively, this level of exactness isn't influenced by the medium in which the message is passed on [8]. Thinks about have appeared that misdirection discovery is roughly the same whether the message is passed on through content (e.g., a court transcript, a Web chat log), a sound recording (e.g., a voicemail, a radio program), or a video (e.g., a cross-examination video).

Even though this could seem shocking given the wealthier detail accessible in the video, exactness tends to be at chance notwithstanding of medium since there are no solid signals to human double-dealing (i.e., there's no Pinocchio's nose). We tend to believe what others say. But the vast, more significant part of the investigation on video-based double-dealing has inspected the verbal substance of a discourse, for illustration, an individual telling a lie, as contradicted to the development and form of a person's body. One of the foremost energizing angles of this uncommon issue is to investigate duplicity that is not based exclusively on lies told with words but instep the total manufacture of verbal and nonverbal behaviors.

Although the rates of discovery are likely compared to other media, the effect of double-dealing by DF can be more prominent than verbal duplicity sense of the supremacy of visual communication for human cognition. DFs not as it altered oral substance, but they too change the optical properties of how the message was passed on, whether this incorporates the development of a person's mouth saying something that they did not, or the behavior of an individual doing something that they did not. The dominance of visual signals in human recognition is well built up. For case, beneath numerous circumstances, people depend more on visual data than other shapes of tactile data, a wonder alluded to as the Colavita visual dominance impact.

Within the basic Colavita worldview, members ought to make speeded responses to an irregular arrangement of sound-related, visual, or varying media jolts. Members are taught to create one reaction to a sound-related target, another reaction to a visual target, and to form both reactions at whatever point the sound-related and visual targets are displayed simultaneously. Members have no issue reacting to the sound and video targets independently, but when they are displayed together, they regularly fall flat to reply to the sound-related targets. It is as in case the visual boosts quench the sound boosts. It is observed that individuals are more likely to review visual messages than verbal messages, and deceiving visual data is more likely to generate wrong recognitions than deceiving verbal substance because of the "realism heuristic," in which individuals are more likely to believe varying media modalities over verbal since the essence encompasses a higher likeness to the real world.

The video was the final frontier—the one that customers may observe and not consequently expect to be faked [9]. But what happens when we learn that a video can be "photoshopped" as effortlessly as pictures can be? Can we accept any media that we see? The rationalist Wear Fallis alludes to this as the epistemic risk of DFs [5]. His contention streams from the control of visual media to carry data, which indicates how much flag is passed on by a message. Because of the dominance of the visual framework, recordings have tall data-carrying potential—that is, we tend to accept what we see in a video, and as a result, recordings have gotten to be the "gold standard" of truth. But as DFs multiply and mindfulness that recordings can be faked spread through the populace, the sum of data that recordings carry to watchers is decreased.

Indeed, if a video is veritable and a watcher would procure genuine convictions, doubt born of DFs would prevent an individual from really accepting what they saw [1,7]. The epistemic risk for Fallis is that DFs will meddle with our capacity to obtain information approximately the world by observing media. The suggestions for our shared understanding of the world and the part that news coverage and other media play in building that world maybe genuinely undermined.

## 9.4 SOCIETAL IMPACT

Shockingly, one of the few observational considers on DFs gives a few early proofs that worryingly bears this philosophical account out. In a ponder looking at the impact of DFs on belief within the news [10], Vaccari and Chadwick found that even though individuals were impossible to be deluded by a DF (at slightest with the innovation they were utilizing), introduction to the DF expanded their instability around media in common. Affirming the most noticeably awful desires, that sense of instability had driven members to diminish their belief in news, much as Fallis's account of epistemic danger predicts.

DFs, moreover, have interpersonal results. As the VR ponders as of now depicted recommend, video DFs have the potential to adjust our recollections and indeed embed bad memories. They can alter a person's demeanors toward the target of the DF. One later ponder uncovered that presentation to a DF delineating a political figure essentially declined participants' states of mind toward that lawmaker. Indeed more worryingly, given social media's capacity to target substance to particular political or statistic bunches, the ponder uncovered that microtargeting the DF to groups most likely to be outraged (e.g., Christians) increased this impact relative to sharing the DF with a common populace.

Even though these suggestions paint a disheartening representation of a future with DF innovation, this takes expecting a moderately inactive media buyer [11, 12]. It is vital to review that people have been adjusting to novel shapes of misdirection for millennia. Individuals tend to trust one another until they have a few reasons to become suspicious or more watchful, a state that Levine alludes to as a belief default. We move out of our belief default when we learn approximately conflicting data, a third party cautions us, or we are taught almost novel tricky procedures. For case, mail spam is much less successful than when it began with developed since individuals are mindful of it.

In the same way, it is conceivable for individuals to create strength to novel shapes of misdirection such as DFs. For illustration, publicizing habitually depends on deceiving visual data (e.g., drink this brew, have wonderful companions; smoke this cigarette, encounter the great outside). Over time, buyers get their watch up and are not tricked by publicizing, in portion since they create a pattern of desires for promoting. Without a doubt, we make desires like this for most media we devour. For illustration, DF innovation is now utilized in Hollywood motion pictures. For example, the depiction of Princess Leia in Star Wars VIII after the performing artist Carrie Fisher had kicked the bucket. Most individuals mark the DF as fiction because they observe an anecdotal motion picture. But, a critical address is whether the visual proof begins to chip absent at the viewers' memory that the performing artist has passed absent, in any case of their information that it could be a motion picture?

However, an imperative hurt we have not considered is the nonconsensual casualty depicted in a DF to be doing or saying something that they did not. One of the foremost common early shapes of DFs is the modification of obscenity, delineating nonconsensual people locks in a sex act that never happened regularly by putting a person's confront on another person's body. Given the control of the visual framework in modifying our convictions as of now portrayed and the impact that such DFs can have on a self-character, the effect on a victim's life can be destroyed. Even though observational inquiry about the date is constrained, it isn't difficult to assume how DFs may be utilized to blackmail, mortify, or annoy casualties.

## 9.5 SUMMARY

In this uncommon issue, we encourage analysts to ponder the social issues encompassing DF innovation. The ponders in this volume do an incredible job of mapping out the inquire about questions, applying hypothesis to the marvel, and making unused instruments to apply to future inquiries. But this ponder is preparatory, and we encourage researchers to construct upon this consider as DF utilize proceeds to develop.

Be that as it may, there's another related wilderness that needs consideration. As of now, when we examine DFs, we are alluding to recorded video. But ML has progressed adequately to empower real-time DFs: AI-powered channels. These channels permit for altering or optimizing the video substance of a videoconference in real-time, such as making a person's eye look show up even though it is pointed at the camera indeed, even though it is suggested somewhere else on the screen. In expansion to overseeing [13] joint consideration in ungainly video settings, other DF channels are being created to optimize for other interpersonal elements, such as warmth or interpersonal fascination. For case, Goodness et al. utilized a real-time medium to improve the sum of grinning [14,15] in dyads, demonstrating that accomplices within the upgraded grinning conditions felt more emphatically after the discussion and used more positive words amid their discussion based on the etymological investigation.

It is basic to note that these downstream impacts happened indeed, even though the members were not mindful of the grinning channel and nearly never recognized. Analysts at the MIT Media research facility are creating "personalized part models" utilizing DF innovation to modify a real-time video stream to permit the speakers to see adaptations of themselves exceeding expectations at talking assignments in a sure way. They are illustrating impacts not as they were on temperament but assignment imagination. This utilizes of AI to adjust one's self-introduction amid videoconferencing could be a frame of AI-mediated communication, which alludes to "interpersonal communication in which a brilliantly specialist works on the sake of a communicator by adjusting, expanding, or producing messages to achieve communication goals."

Even though DF innovation can weaken our belief in media or erroneously impact our convictions approximately the world, it may end up more commonplace and ordinary as individuals utilize DF innovation to move forward their day-to-day communication. As the specified discourse clarifies and the articles in this uncommon issue highlight, there are numerous imperative mental, social, and moral issues that require imaginative and cautious observational examinations of the social effect of DF advances.

## REFERENCES

[1] Tolosana R, Vera-Rodriguez R, Fierrez J, et al. DFs and beyond: A survey of face manipulation and fake detection. Information Fusion 2020; 64: 131–148.

[2] Fox J, & Bailenson JN. Virtual self-modeling: The effects of vicarious reinforcement and identification on exercise behaviors. Media Psychology 2009; 12: 1–25.

[3] Garry M, & Wade KA. Actually, a picture is worth less than 45 words: Narratives produce more false memories than photographs do. Psychonomic Bulletin & Review 2005; 12: 359–366.

[4] Ahmed S. Who inadvertently shares DFs? Analyzing the role of political interest, cognitive ability, and social network size. Telematics and Informatics 2021; 57: 101508.

[5] Doffman Z. Chinese DF app ZAO goes viral, privacy of millions 'at risk'. Forbes Magazine. 2019. www .forbes.com/sites/zakdoffman/2019/09/02/chinese-best-ever-DF-app-zao-sparks-huge-faceapp-like-privacy-storm/?sh=2951ebb88470 (accessed Jan. 27, 2021).

[6] Ahn SJ, & Bailenson J. Self-endorsed advertisements: When the self persuades the self. Journal of Marketing Theory and Practice 2014; 22: 135–136.

[7] Levine TR. (2019) *Duped: Truth-default Theory and the Social Science of Lying and Deception.* Tuscaloosa, AL: University Alabama Press.

[8] Bond Jr CF, & DePaulo BM. Accuracy of deception judgments. Personality and Social Psychology Review 2006; 10: 214–234.

[9] Segovia KY, & Bailenson JN. Virtually true: Children's acquisition of false memories in virtual reality. MediaPsychology 2009; 12: 371–393.

[10] Goodfellow I. Nips 2016 tutorial: GANs 2016; arXiv preprint arXiv:1701.00160. Social Impact of DFS.

[11] Hancock JT, Woodworth MT, & Goorha S. See no evil: The effect of communication medium and motivation on deception detection. Group Decision Negotiation 2010; 19: 327–343.

[12] Suwajanakorn S, Seitz SM, & Kemelmacher-Shlizerman I. Synthesizing Obama: Learning lip sync from audio. ACM Transactions on Graphics (ToG) 2017; 36: 1–13.

[13] Mahbub Md. K, Biswas M, Gaur L, Alenezi F, & Santosh K. Deep features to detect pulmonary abnormalities in chest X-rays due to infectious disease X: Covid-19, pneumonia, and tuberculosis. Information Sciences 2022; 592: 389–401. https://doi.org/10.1016/J.INS.2022.01.062.

[14] Sharma S, Singh G, Gaur L, & Sharma R. Does psychological distance and religiosity influence fraudulent customer behavior? International Journal of Consumer Studies 2022. 10.1111/ijcs.12773.

[15] Zaman N & Gaur L. *Approaches and Applications of Deep Learning in Virtual Medical Care.* IGI Global. 2022. doi:10.4018/978-1-7998-8929-8.ch002

# 10 Fake News Detection Using Machine Learning

*Sonali Raturi, Amit Kumar Mishra, and Srabanti Maji*

## CONTENTS

## 10.1 INTRODUCTION

We are living in a society where people usually rely on social media principles where many people are probable to look up and get news or posts from social media, not from conventional news such as newspapers. False news refers to poor-quality news that contains false news which is intentionally created. The vast spread of fake news day by day has the ability for tremendous bad effects on the society or any individual [1]. Fake news is written to mislead the readers so that they could believe the false information that is intentionally generated, which makes it hard to detect fake news dependent on the report contents only; hence, we need to involve reserved information [2] that could be the user's social involvements on social media which help to form a conclusion.

DOI: 10.1201/9781003231493-10

## 10.2 REASONS USING SOCIAL MEDIA FOR FAKE NEWS

In the case of social media, it should be provided in a timely fashion and not that much expensive for consumers to consume news rather than other traditional news media such as newspapers. Social media makes it easy to share news further or comment on, and we can consider the update with the help of other readers in an easier fashion.

However, news articles are [3] produced online because it is less expensive and faster to release news through social media. These are obtained online for different purposes such as political and financial gain. During this pandemic situation, gossip travels at a faster speed. Fake data is spreading across social media along with remedies. The way to differentiate real news with misinformation is by associating diverse properties and theories in media, i.e., conventional as well as social media. Now, the drawbacks in the fake news prediction will be defined and the methods will be reviewed. Next, the datasets that will be used in this method and the evaluation of a new model used by the existing methods will be defined. There are mainly two basic features: authenticity and intent. First, false evidence can be verified. Second, it is generated to mislead the consumers with dishonest intentions.

## 10.3 REASONS TO SPREAD FAKE NEWS

Fake news could be rumors that are generally not generated from any news events, only for political gain or any financial gain. Fake news could be misinformation that is generated unpremeditated. Fake news could be produced by fun or to hustle a specific person. Recently, fake news is dynamic as changing its phase from traditional media to social media or online news. Here are two components that make users endangered to false news or posts:

Naive Realism: In this, users start believing that their viewpoints for reality are the only views that are accurate [4], and those whose viewpoints vary are considered as prejudiced.

Confirmation Bias: In this, users believe to receive only that information that their existing views are confirmed.

## 10.4 VENOMOUS ACCOUNTS ON SOCIAL MEDIA FOR ADVOCACY

The major reason for venomous accounts could be the cost-effectiveness of creating an account on social media. It is less expensive to create bots online for social media. A bot could be an account on social media and is managed by different computer algorithms so that it can produce content and link with bots or people automatically on social media [5]. Social bots are said to venomous entities when it is designed with the specific purpose, basically to harm, such as to spread or manipulate hoax news on social media. People start believing in hoax news on account of the following factors:

Due to the credibility on social media, which means users are likely to consider a source of fake news as credible if others consider the same source as credible. And they do so when there is not enough information available to decide whether the source is fake or real, or the truthfulness of any source.

Due to the frequency heuristic, which means users [6] naturally start supporting that information which they hear time and again even it could be fake news.

## 10.5  FAKE NEWS DETECTION METHODS

It is a way of determining fake news. And this work is based on detecting fake news on social media using Machine Learning (ML). There are several different algorithms of ML, including Naïve Bayes and RNN [7]. Using these proposed algorithms, we could generate a tool for determining this faux news on social media.

## 10.6  LINEAR REGRESSION

It is a method that models a final value based on independent predictors. This technique is a supervised ML algorithm. The **regression task is done in this algorithm**. The application of this technique is forecasting. This method is different based on the number of independent values and the bond between the dependent and independent values [8].

## 10.7  RANDOM FOREST

Random forest is made up of a vast numeral of decision trees. A separate tree is an algorithm expelled out a class prediction [9]. Same as how stocks and bonds combined to build a portfolio that is larger than the total. Some trees may be right, or others may be erroneous, so trees can move the proper path. So, the requirements for proper functioning of random forest are as follows:

Required some genuine signal in features so that models constructed through those features can perform better than random estimation [10].The predictions performed by single trees must have low correlations with another.

## 10.8  DECISION TREE

It is the fundamental block of the random forest design. In addition, they are extremely instinctive.

For instance, it is a lot easier to comprehend exactly how does a decision tree perform out of the instance. Suppose that our datasets have two 1s and five 0s and we want to classify. This can be performed with features as red color vs. blue color as well as whether the remark is emphasized or not. Therefore, is it possible? Color appears to be a feature to divide through the medium like all, but few zeroes are represented as blue. Consequently, we can say that 'Does this color show as red?' Assume a node within a tree in the same way as the point where the trail is divided into two, i.e., Yes branch and No branch. The No branch that is in blue is all 0s, and another trail will be able to divide beyond [11,12]. The ones represent the yes, and the zero represent as correct sub-trail.

## 10.9   GRADIENT BOOSTING CLASSIFIER

For solving the problems of classification and regression, this ML technique is used. This is relevant to the decision tree algorithm; whenever the decision tree is producing the performance like a weak learner, then the algorithm is known as gradient-boosted trees. It creates the model in the stage-wise pattern [13].

## 10.10   PASSIVE-AGGRESSIVE CLASSIFIER

This ML algorithm may be useful for certain applications. It is used for large-scale learning. In this, the data is serial, and ML is updated one by one where the whole training data is used at once.

How Passive-Aggressive classifier works:

Passive: If the prediction is accurate, then do not change the data.

Aggressive: If the prediction is inaccurate, then changes can be done to the model.

## 10.11   RELATED WORK

The following is the literature review:

Mykhalio et al. (2017) advanced a simple method for fake news detection along with the consumption of Naïve Bayes classifier. For this, he has used BuzzFeed News; he has used it to know and test the Naïve Bayes classifier. Cody et al. (2017) recommended a technique that automates fake news recognition; it works on Twitter. They applied this technique to the source of Twitter and accessed the data for automating false news detection from BuzzFeed's fake news dataset on Twitter. Marco et al. (2017) advanced a paper. In this paper, they narrated how social networks and gadgets using and studying different ML strategies could be used for false news detection. They used and accomplished this method of fake news detection inside of a Facebook Messenger bot and initiated it with other applications. Rishabh et al. (2015) accomplished three algorithms of ML including Naïve Bayes and others as clustering on some of the features. These features can be a degree of a tweet or like followers, any Spam words generated intentionally, comments of users, and hashtags used on social media. Saranya et al. (2018) presented a concept where they used a higher-up framework that can detect false information content. At first, they have drawn out the content material having capability functions using Twitter API. And then, all these functions are operated at once with some analysis of Twitter; after this, it converses searching of the picture, and authentication of the false news is used by different algorithms; this authentication is done for class and analysis. Shloka (2017) carried out a concept in which NLP is applicable to trip on false information. In this, he has applied time, some concepts of bigrams, and also used context-free grammar detection in his concept. Marco et al. (2018) presented an ML fake news detection method within a Facebook Messenger chatbot. Also, they applied this method with a physical-world application. They combined social-based and content-based methods that are dependent upon a threshold rule. Stefan et al. (2018) presented a weakly supervised approach. This approach impulsive collects a large amount but contains a heavy noisy training dataset. They used Weak Supervision, ML, and Classification. Monther et al. (2018) proposed that clickbait interferes with fake news, having the potential that a user will spot helpful information. They used classification in their approach. Sagar et al. (2017) presented a model that is dependent upon two new features: inspection of language and the recognition of spam tweets. They used statistical NLP in their model and also ML. Lourdes et al. (2010) proposed well-organized faux detection system that depends on a classifier that merges the latest link-based features and using these features with language model (LM)-based ones using content analysis. Ye et al. (2019) presented a Deep Learning help of Natural Language Contents Estimation System. This system detects fake news that determines false information using NLP. Vanya et al. (2020) proposed a fake news detection system to categorize the news headlines or text as false or not false by evaluating the news headlines according to the labels using ML, NLP, and k-nearest neighbor. Jasmine et al. (2020) proposed a false news detection technique that used various classification methods. They applied classification methods such as Passive-Aggressive classifier, SVM, and Naïve Bayes. The outcome of SVM classifier is 95% precision and the method used for feature extraction is TF-IDF. Mykhailo et al. (2020) presented a model where they applied the Naive Bayes classifier. Here, this model was executed as a software system, and a dataset of Facebook news posts is used for testing. A classification accuracy of 74% was achieved on the test data. Alia et al. (2018) proposed a Rumor Tracking System that used a web scraping method. This model discovers sources on the sites and confirms the content using an Information Matching Algorithm. Youngkyung Seo et al. (2015) presented a false news detection system that is dependent on deep learning and predicts whether the post is fake or real using grammatical transformation. This system consists of some layers: matching layers, inference layers, embedding layers, and context generation layers. We summarized the literature review in tabular format as well (Table 10.1).

## 10.12  OBJECTIVE

The main objective of this model is to recognize false news problems on social media, so people can easily differentiate between fake news and real news. This model used Natural Language processing and a Passive-Aggressive classifier and obtained accuracy. The spread of false news gives a negative impact on people [14,15,16]. Therefore, fake news detection is required to reduce the spread of such irrelevant news. Using the TF-IDF to transform the text into a meaningful depiction of numbers is used for prediction with ML algorithms.

We summarized our objective here:

The main objective of this model is to recognize false news problems on social media so people can easily differentiate between fake news and real news. This

**TABLE 10.1**
**Summary of Literature Survey**

| S. No. | Author | Approach | Result |
|---|---|---|---|
| 1 | Kyeong-Hwan Kim et al. (2017) | Sentence matching, Deep learning, NLP | A Korean fake news detector that is created and can be updated by human judgment |
| 2 | Amitabha Dey et al. (2017) | Polarization, Linguistic analysis, KNN-algorithm, classification | A framework that can be used to make better decisions |
| 3 | Marco L. Della Vedova et al. (2017) | Combined social-based and content-based techniques that are based upon threshold rule | A Machine Learning fake news detection that is used within a Facebook Messenger |
| 4 | Stefan Helmstetter et al. (2015) | Weak Supervision, Machine Learning | A weakly supervised approach. Here, it collects large data but a noisy training dataset. |
| 5 | Monther Aldwairi et al. (2018) | Classification | A model with the ability of a user to discern useful information |
| 6 | Palagati Bhanu, Prakash Reddy et al. (2017) | NLP, random forest, KNN, SVM, Decision tree, Naïve Bayes | Fake news detector using the multinomial voting algorithm |
| 7 | Sagar Gharge et al. (2018) | Statistical NLP, Machine Learning | A technique dependent on two principles: the detection of fake tweets and another dependent on the analysis of language |
| 8 | Burak et al. (2018) | Natural language processing | A model for NER algorithm |
| 9 | Alina Campan et al. (2018) | Information diffusion, Influence maximization | Presented how fake news spread in the current online social networks |
| 10 | Bhavika Bhutani et al. (2017) | Naive Bayes, Random Forest | Fake news detection system which includes sentiment analysis to improve the accuracy |
| 11 | Lourdes Araujo et al. (2010) | Content analysis | Fake news detection model that used link-based features with language model-based |
| 12 | Ye-Chan Ahn et al. (2019) | Natural Language Processing | Fake news detection system to judge such inaccurate information using Natural Language Contents Evaluation |
| 13 | Va Vanya Tiwari et al. (2019) | NLP, KNN, Machine learning | Fake news detector that classifies news headlines or text as fake or not fake by analyzing the news headlines with labels |

model used Natural Language processing and a Passive-Aggressive classifier and find the accuracy.

The spread of false news gives a negative impact on people. Therefore, fake news detection is required to reduce [17,18,19] the spread of inappropriate news.

Using the TF-IDF to transform the text into a meaningful depiction of numbers is used for prediction with machine learning algorithms.

## 10.13  METHODOLOGY

Our suggested system intends to evaluate the classification suing Passive-Aggressive classifier using the news-related datasets. The resulting dataset is split into two subcategories. First, the Training set used 80% of the dataset, and second, the Test set used 20% of the dataset. Dataset collection, data pre-processing, and classification are applied to the model.

## 10.14  DATASET

This model utilized the dataset which is collected from Kaggle. This dataset is news-related which includes ID, title, author, and text, i.e., subject of the news in conjunction with the label [20,21,22] of true and false values, where missing values are omitted. The final dataset is imperturbable of 18,285 posts with the label, a little labeled as fake and certain labeled as real. Additional information related to the dataset is provided in Table 10.2. The news texts were evaluated to the pre-processing tasks that are included in the data pre-processing section. Additionally, knowledge from the data has been collected to build a better understanding, utilizing the ML technique.

## 10.15  DATA PRE-PROCESSING

This section covers tokenization, lemmatization, removal of stop words, removal of punctuation marks, null checkers, and preparation of the data to be delivered to the model to execute further steps. Data cleaning is the process in which data is being prepared for evaluation, which is done by removing irrelevant or inappropriate data or altering the data. That data could be inappropriate, inadequate, or not properly

**TABLE 10.2**
**Dataset**

| Id | Title | Author | Text | Label |
|----|-------|--------|------|-------|
| 0 | House Dem Aide: | Darrell Lucus | House Dem Aide: | 1 |
| 1 | FLYNN: Hillary | Daniel J. Flynn | **Ever get the** | 0 |
| 2 | Why the Truth | Consortiumnews.com | **Elton print out** | 1 |
| 3 | 15 Civilians Killed | Jessica Purkiss | **Videos 15 Civilians** | 1 |
| 4 | Iranian woman | Howard Portnoy | **Print An Iranian woman** | 1 |

configured [23,24,25]. Since it provides inaccurate results, the data used here is not accurate to examine data. There are various techniques for cleaning the data that will vary depending on how it is stored with the results. Here, a model will be created that can foretell the truthfulness of real-time news. Lemmatization and tokenization are applied using the Natural Language Tool Kit (NLTK). Lemmatization is the process of gathering the various modified forms of a word so that they could be examined as an individual item. Hence, it links words with common meaning to a single word. Tokenization is a key step in Natural Language Processing methods such as Count Vectorizer as well as Transformers. It is a way of splitting a chunk of text into smaller units referred to as tokens.

## 10.16  MODEL EVALUATION

After the data pre-processing, the dataset is divided into two, i.e., test data and training data, and acquired the accuracy using Passive-Aggressive classifier. Natural Language Processing uses statistical, ML, deep learning, and computational linguistics. Together, it allows the process of human language in the form of text or voice [26,27,28]. NLP executes programs that convert the text from one language to another language. Passive-Aggressive classifier is also called an online algorithm. We used this algorithm when we have a big stream of data.

Here, if prediction then apply prediction multiply with weight vector as:

$$d^T w > 0 \tag{10.1}$$

If positive, then y = +1
If negative, then y = −1

where y = observe true classes, when it is less than 1, then we represent it by adding a small portion of D, that is the vector we received and the weight vector. Aggressive gives the loss that we have received.

## 10.17  RESULT AND DISCUSSIONS

We used the TF-IDF vectorizer to obtain the features and approved them to the classifier. As in this model, Passive-Aggressive classifier is applied using tokenization and

**TABLE 10.3**
**Data Cleaning**

| ID | Label |
|----|-------|
| 0  | 1     |
| 1  | 0     |
| 2  | 1     |
| 3  | 1     |
| 4  | 1     |

**TABLE 10.4**
**Accuracy**

| Accuracy | True values | False values |
|----------|-------------|--------------|
| 95%      | 43.3%       | 56.7%        |

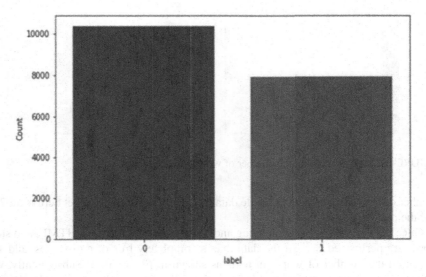

**FIGURE 10.1** Visualization of the fake and true dataset.

lemmatization with Natural Language Processing and obtained the accuracy. This model in conjunction with the accuracy provides an approximation of the best performance technique. Natural Language Processing (NLP) and its numerous tools are used for data cleaning (Table 10.3). It is a significant portion of text classification. The accuracy we get, as in Table 10.4, plainly invented that the Passive-Aggressive classifier algorithm is performing better with an accuracy of 95%.

Dataset, representing news, are collected from Kaggle. The dataset contains titles, author, and text along with the label, i.e., '0' and '1', 'false' and 'true', respectively. It contains news-related data. The missing values are omitted from the dataset. More description about the dataset is described in Table 10.2. The dataset we have used contains 56.7% fake data and 43.3% true data, as shown in Table 10.4. The experiment is carried out using the Python platform.

In the pre-processing, we have removed all the HTML, punctuation marks, and English stop words. The ML algorithm we have used in our model is the Passive-Aggressive algorithm for classification [29,30,31]. This algorithm is implemented by using the scikit-learn python package. An experiment was performed on a 64-bit processing system. Missing values are removed by deleting columns that contain null values as in Table 10.2. Visualization of data is done in Figure 10.1. It shows the

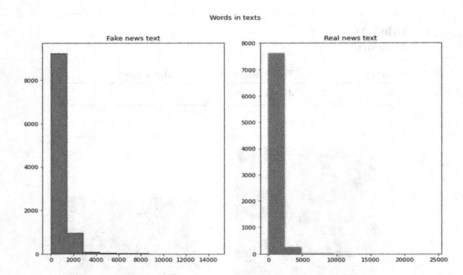

**FIGURE 10.2**   The graph on the number of words in each text.

number of fake and real data in single datasets. So, the fake data we get here is 56.7% and the real data is 43.3%.

Once the processes of data cleaning and removal of punctuations, HTML, and stop words are performed, we get the data that is completely free of null values, and we measured the number of words in texts as shown in Figure 10.2. Subsequently, we split the dataset into test data and training data. The Passive-Aggressive classifier is applied to the resulting dataset [32,33,34].

As shown in Table 10.4, we pulled out data pre-processing using Natural Language Processing with [35,36,37] Passive-Aggressive classifier with an accuracy of 95%.

Accuracy is performed for assessing the classification models. Confidentially, an accuracy is the proportion of forecasts our model obtained correctly. Officially, an accuracy formula is just as mentioned in the following:

$$Accuracy = \frac{\text{Number of correct predictions}}{\text{Total number of predictions}} \tag{10.2}$$

The equation to measure accuracy in terms of positives and negatives is described in the following:

$$Accuracy = \frac{TP + TN}{TP + TN + FP + FN} \tag{10.3}$$

where TP is True Positives, FP is False Positives, FN is False Negatives, and TN is True Negatives.

We obtained the accuracy of the techniques and if their average is nearly close to the true value that is being stated.

## 10.18   SUMMARY

The work to classify fake news manually need in-depth knowledge of expertise and domain to recognize irregularities in the text. In this research, we generate a model that detects fakes news with the use of NLP and Passive-Aggressive classifier. The data we used in our work is collected through the Kaggle. The research is to identify patterns in text that differentiate fake news from real news. We pulled out different data cleaning using Natural Language Processing and Passive-Aggressive classifier for classification with an accuracy of 95%. False news detection has many issues that need the awareness of researchers. For instance, we need to recognize the key elements to reduce the spread of fake news. ML methods can be used to define the elements involved in the growth of false news. In addition, false news detection with deep learning can be another future direction using various feature extraction.

## REFERENCES

[1] Araujo, L. and Martinez, R. J. (2010). Web Spam Detection: New Classification Features Based on Qualified Link Analysis and Language Models. IEEE Transactions on Information Forensics and Security, 581–590.

[2] Ahn, Y. and Jeong, C. (2019). Natural Language Contents Evaluation System for Detecting Fake News using Deep Learning. 16th International Joint Conference on Computer Science and Software Engineering (JCSSE).

[3] Buntain, C. and Golbeck, J. (2017). Automatically Identifying Fake News in PopularTwitterThreads. IEEE International Conference on Smart Cloud.

[4] Chin, P.-Y., Choo, K. K. R., and Evans, N. (2015). Exploring factors influencing the use of enterprise social networks in multinational professional service firms. Journal of Organizational Computing and Electronic Commerce, 25, 289–315.

[5] Davis, C., Ferrara, E., Flammini, A., and Varol, O. (2016). The rise of social bots. Communications of the ACM, 96–104.

[6] Granik, M. and Mesyura, V. (2017). Fake News Detection Using Bayes Classifier, IEEE First Ukraine Conference on Electrical and Computer Engineering (UKRCON).

[7] Gupta, A. and Kaushal, R. (2015). Improving Spam Detection in Online Social Networks, 978-1-4799-7171.

[8] Gilda, S. (2017). Evaluating Machine Learning Algorithms for Fake News Detection. IEEE 15th Student Conference on Research Development (SCOReD).

[9] Granik, M. and Mesyura, V. (2017). Fake News Detection Using Naive Bayes Classifier. IEEE First Ukraine Conference on Electrical and Computer Engineering (UKRCON), 900–903.

[10] Chavan, M. and Gharge, S. (2017). An integrated approach for malicious tweets detection using NLP. 2017 International Conference on Inventive Communication and Computational Technologies (ICICCT).

[11] Helmstetter, S. and Paulheim, H. (2018). Weakly Supervised Learning for Fake News Detection on Twitter. IEEE/ACM International Conference on Advances in Social Networks Analysis and Mining (ASONAM), 274–277.

[12] Chen, M. and Krishanan, S. (2018). Identifying Tweets with Fake News. IEEE Information Reuse and Integration for Data Science.

[13] Ali, A. and Monther, A. (2018). Detecting Fake News in Social Media Networks, 9th International Networks. 9th International Conference on Emerging Ubiquitous Systems and Pervasive Networks (EUSPN).

[14] Ghani, V., Mochamad, A., and Setijadi, P., A. (2015). Design and Implementation of Natural Language Processing with Syntax and Semantic Analysis for Extract Traffic Conditions from Social Media Data. IEEE 5th International Conference on System Engineering and Technology.

[15] Nickerson, R. S. (1998). Confirmation bias: A ubiquitous phenomenon in many guises. Review of General Psychology, 2(2), 175.

[16] Patil, R. and Shaikh (2020). Fake News Detection using Machine Learning. IEEE International Symposium on Sustainable Energy, Signal Processing and Cyber Security (ISSSC), 1–5.

[17] Samreen, A., Ahmad, A., and Zeshan, F. (2020). Searching for Truth in the Post-Truth Age. 3rd International Conference on Advancements in Computational Sciences (ICACS), 1–5.

[18] Seo, Y. and Jeong, C. (2018). FaGoN: Fake News Detection Model Using Grammatic Transformation on Neural Network. Thirteenth International Conference on Knowledge, Information and Creativity Support Systems (KICSS), 1–5.

[19] Tiwari, V., Lennon, R. G., and Dowling T. (2020). Not Everything You Read Is True! Fake News Detection using Machine learning Algorithms. 31st Irish Signals and Systems Conference (ISSC), 1–4.

[20] Ballarin, G., de Massimo, A. L., Moret, S., Vendova, M. L. D., and Tacchini, E. (2017). Automatic Online Fake News Detection Combining Content and Social Signals, 2305–7254.

[21] Ballarin, G., de Alfaro, L., DiPierro, M., Moret, S., Vedova, D. M. L., and Tacchini, E. (2018). Automatic Online Fake News Detection Combining Content and Social Signals. Conference of Open Innovations Association (FRUCT), 272–279.

[22] Brown, T., Ward, A., Ross, L., Reed, E., and Turiel, E. (1997). Naive realism in everyday life: Implications for social conflict and misunderstanding. Values and Knowledge, 103–135. https://web.mit.edu/curhan/www/docs/Articles/15341_Readi ngs/Negotiation_and_Conflict_Management/Ross_Ward_Naive_Realism.pdf

[23] Juan, C., Jiebo, L., Yongdong, Z., and Zhiwei, J. (2016). News verification by exploiting conflicting social viewpoints in microblogs. In *AAAI'16*.

[24] Anshu, K., Gaur, L., and Khazanchi, D. (2017). "Evaluating satisfaction level of grocery E-retailers using intuitionistic fuzzy TOPSIS and ECCSI model," International Conference on Infocom Technologies and Unmanned Systems (Trends and Future Directions) (ICTUS), pp. 276–284. doi:10.1109/ICTUS.2017.8286019

[25] Gaur, L. and Anshu, K. (2018). Consumer preference analysis for websites using e-TailQ and AHP. International Journal of Engineering & Technology, 7(2.11), 14–20.

[26] Rana, J., Gaur, L., Singh, G., Awan, U., and Rasheed, M.I. (2021). Reinforcing customer journey through artificial intelligence: A review and research agenda. International Journal of Emerging Markets, Vol. ahead-of-print (No. ahead-of-print). https://doi.org/10.1108/IJOEM-08-2021-1214

[27] Gaur, L., Singh, G., Solanki, A., Jhanjhi, N. Z., Bhatia, U., Sharma, S., … and Kim, W. (2021). Disposition of youth in predicting sustainable development goals using the neuro-fuzzy and random forest algorithms. Human-Centric Computing and Information Sciences, 11, NA.

[28] Singh, G., Kumar, B., Gaur, L., and Tyagi, A. (2019). "Comparison between Multinomial and Bernoulli Naïve Bayes for Text Classification," 2019 International Conference on Automation, Computational and Technology Management (ICACTM), pp. 593–596. doi:10.1109/ICACTM.2019.8776800

[29] Gaur, L., Agarwal, V., and Anshu, K. (2020), "Fuzzy DEMATEL Approach to Identify the Factors Influencing Efficiency of Indian Retail," Strategic System Assurance and

Business Analytics. Asset Analytics (Performance and Safety Management). Springer, Singapore. https://doi.org/10.1007/978-981-15-3647-2_

[30] Gaur, L., Afaq, A., Singh, G., and Dwivedi, Y.K. (2021). Role of artificial intelligence and robotics to foster the touchless travel during a pandemic: A review and research agenda. International Journal of Contemporary Hospitality Management, 33(11), 4079–4098. https://doi.org/10.1108/IJCHM-11-2020-1246

[31] Sharma, S., Singh, G., Gaur, L., and Sharma, R. (2022). Does psychological distance and religiosity influence fraudulent customer behaviour? International Journal of Consumer Studies. doi:10.1111/ijcs.12773

[32] Sahu, G., Gaur, L., and Singh, G. (2021). Applying niche and gratification theory approach to examine the users' indulgence towards over-the-top platforms and conventional TV. Telematics and Informatics, 65. doi:10.1016/j.tele.2021.101713

[33] Ramakrishnan, R., Gaur, L., and Singh, G. (2016). Feasibility and efficacy of BLE beacon IoT devices in inventory management at the shop floor. International Journal of Electrical and Computer Engineering, 6(5), 2362–2368. doi:10.11591/ijece. v6i5.10807

[34] Afaq, A., Gaur, L., Singh, G., and Dhir, A. (2021). COVID-19: Transforming air passengers' behaviour and reshaping their expectations towards the airline industry. Tourism Recreation Research. doi:10.1080/02508281.2021.2008211

[35] Mahbub, Md. K., Biswas, M., Gaur, L., Alenezi, F., and Santosh, K. (2022). Deep features to detect pulmonary abnormalities in chest X-rays due to infectious disease X: Covid-19, pneumonia, and tuberculosis. Information Sciences, 592, 389–401. https://doi.org/10.1016/J.INS.2022.01.062

[36] Sharma, S., Singh, G., Gaur, L., & Sharma, R. (2022). Does psychological distance and religiosity influence fraudulent customer behavior? International Journal of Consumer Studies. 10.1111/ijcs.12773.

[37] Zaman, N., & Gaur, L. (2022). *Approaches and Applications of Deep Learning in Virtual Medical Care*. IGI. doi:10.4018/978-1-7998-8929-8.ch002

# 11 Future of DeepFakes and Ectypes

*Loveleen Gaur, Mansi Ratta, and Adesh Gaur*

## CONTENTS

## 11.1 INTRODUCTION

A professor from Northeastern University started a company for recreating voices. It aims to provide customized voices to people who cannot speak. Even an ordinary person can get their voice customized if they risk losing it in the future. This pioneering project can give people an essential part of their identity back [1]. In one instance, a UK energy company's chief executive has tricked into wiring 200,000 euros to a Hungarian supplier because he believed his boss was instructing him to do so. Such instances make DeepFakes (DFs) unsafe for the society and its people. The real threat is the use of this technology to spread disinformation. The ethical implications and considerations for technology such as DF are vast. Imagine this: a person is charged with a crime and finds a video from surveillance footage in a completely different city. The footage is then put through a DF process to put the person's face and body into the footage. The innocent person will straight away get charged for it. Or what if phone calls could be manufactured with the exact voiceprint of a different person [2]. That could lead to identity theft, fraud, and so much more. We have seen DFs hold the potential to cast doubt on the legitimacy of any form of digital media. It makes it hard to detect what is real and what is fake.

DOI: 10.1201/9781003231493-11

Two years ago, a consortium of more than 100 tech companies, including AWS, Facebook, and Microsoft, created a DF detection challenge offering $1 million for anybody to make an effective way to detect DFs. Another idea that is being hit around is some form of digital watermark issued and stored using a blockchain. When the digital asset is created, it is assigned a unique ID [3]. This ID is like a fingerprint generated from the original. This could then be used to verify the authenticity of that asset later or uncover fakes. It is expected that there will be two main streams of future DF technology. One side will enhance its use and believability of it [4]. The other will be detecting what a DF is and what isn't. Both will be equally important.

## 11.2  DEEPFAKES AND REALITY

The line between the real and digitally unreal is getting blurred. At the same time, it unlocks new forms of creativity and entertainment and fraud and propaganda. Some lawmakers worry that the DFs could be used to attack democracy. Imagine a video appearing on election day showing a candidate in a compromising position. There might not be time for rigorous investigation by police or the press, and DF detection technology is still a work in progress. By the time the truth came to light, it could be too late. On the brighter side, it allows new forms of creativity. Social media is thrumming with examples of DFs made for fun. Like a series in which Tom Cruise appears to practice his golf swing and play guitar [5]. It has a future in ordinarily being used in commercials and corporate training videos. This technology is making its way to our phones and social networks.

A startup called Rosebud has made apps that can transform your age in a selfie or transfer your facial expressions onto the face of Leonardo DiCaprio. All this stuff that seems natural can make a person feel a little icky. People worry that in the era of DFs, the truth will be lost forever. Yet we can also argue that we have been living in a post-reality digital world for some time already. Since the advent of Photoshop in the 1990s, people have gotten used to the idea that images can be faked convincingly. The world hasn't exactly ended. We just know not to treat a photo of an alien or the Loch Ness Monster as a definitive proof [6]. New laws and detection technology may eventually rein in some of the darker sides of DFs. But most of the adaptation will come from us, humans. We are used to the idea that photos can be manipulated, and we look for other signs of trustworthiness, like the source or different contexts. But we'll have to develop new norms for a world where synthetic media is everywhere and learn to live with DFs.

DFs can cause total manipulation of an audience's viewpoints. These viewpoints can be about a person's buying choices, voting choices, what they want, and what they don't want. And it is so subtle that the audience won't even know that they have been directed into buying a thing or voting for someone [7]. In political scenarios, DFs have the potential to manipulate undecided voters into voting for a specific candidate easily.

## 11.3 FORGERY AND ECTYPES

Since the past few decades, we've seen people imitating original works by creating duplicates or replicas. These works may include imitating a famous photograph, creating a fake copy of a well-known painting, or even copying a popular pottery design without mentioning the status of its unoriginality and authenticity. If I recreate the oil painting "The starry Nights" by Vincent Van Gogh and sign it like an original work stating that the former painter paints it, it would be a clear, unauthentic way of selling the painting. Calling a fake copy an original is unethical [8]. Taking inspiration from someone else's work and recreating it with required credits or transparency is the right way to do things. That's where the word ectypes enter. It simply refers to copy work but is somewhat distinguished from the actual work.

An example could better explain ectypes. A couple of years ago, Microsoft, associated with the Rembrandt House Museum, produced art that blurs the line between original and unoriginal work. An Artificial Intelligence (AI) system was made to have a painting inspired by Rembrandt's previous pieces of work. It identified the most common features in his original paintings and created a piece keeping minor details about Rembrandt's paintings in mind. This work is not an original piece of Rembrandt nor a fake copy [9]. This is where the word ectypes can be used. Being an ectype makes it ethical and clears the authenticity status of a work. It can be an audio, photo, or even video.

Whereas using the term ectypes as an identity of work is one solution to the problem of inauthentic behavior caused by DFs. Other ways should also be available, for example, to detect fake circulated videos of politicians before it creates a haphazard atmosphere among the audience. As time passes, our future seems to have increased applications of DF technology [10]. With this technology becoming common in coming years, the demand for an effective solution also grows. We, as a society, have been struggling with forged and manipulated images for a long time now. And today, there are many practical solutions to this problem.

## 11.4 IMAGE FORGERY DETECTOR WITH DEEPFAKES

For example, an "Image Forgery Detector" by Scorto Corporation is a business entirely focused on identifying forged images. They classify the photos provided by customers as developed, suspicious, and authentic. Similarly, many other solutions exist in the promising market. Therefore, in the coming years, with the right kind of techniques and algorithms, there will possibly be an effective solution for the dark side of DFs. In recent years, a lot of research has been done in this area. One of them is a tool created by Microsoft [11]. This tool takes photos or videos as input and provides a confidence score that indicates whether the picture/video is forged. This tool identifies the blended areas in a picture/video which quickly go unnoticed by a person.

Another example is the research by Binghamton University and Intel, where they formed a detection system that helps in identifying the model used alongside the detection of the manipulated photo/video. These tools can only provide help to some extent as they are not always accurate. Also, with time, there is continuous updation in forming a DF. These advancements require robust tools and solutions as well.

Therefore, as the applications and methods of this technology increase, solid solutions are also expected to negate the negative side of DFs.

## 11.5   LEGAL ISSUES WITH DEEPFAKES AND FUTURE STRATEGIES (PROPERTY RIGHTS)

**(Are Property Rights Enough for Combating DF in the Future?)**

By this point, we have established that there's a downside that comes along with some of the DF applications. It is capable of violating our protection rights and misusing any individual's data by manipulating its features. A famous example is the creation of pornographic videos using women's facial pictures. While there are quite a few flaws in the usage of DFs in our society, the first concern arises regarding a person's data rights. Is the creator of a certain DF even allowed to use the data that originally belongs to someone else? Is he given the right to manipulate it? These are the questions that a creator needs to keep in mind before creating a DF. In 2019, World Intellectual Property Organization (WIPO) came up with a draft regarding property rights in AI, where they have included a subsection for DFs. It has addressed the issues regarding intellectual property rights caused by this technology [12]. It has mentioned that the copyrights of a certain DF belong to its creator once they have received the authorization of rights from the person whose data is being used (audio/photo/video). It is so because the idea and innovation belong to the creator, and he should be given credit for it. Also, if the content created intends to show the person (whose data is being used) in a bad light, then the creator should not be assigned any kind of rights to the property. Whereas it also states that the issues with this technology cannot be solved just by creating a copyright framework. The privacy issues and the power to manage some other person's image or status in public cannot be just limited to the copyright policies.

Under the EU, General Data Protection Regulation for European Union ensures that the personal data used to create a DF should be genuine and accurate [13]. In case it is found to be old or inaccurate, then the creator is supposed to remove or correct it within time. It also ensures complete removal of the DF content if it is irrelevant or misleading. Besides guaranteeing the authenticity regarding data, this law gives power to the victim of the DF to practice their right to erase the content without any delay. These regulations make DF not so bad for the European residents. Such rules and regulations are essential if we want to maintain a better relationship with DFs in the future.

## 11.6   FUTURE STRATEGIES: THROUGH ORGANIZATIONAL ASPECTS

Do corporate people understand these AI capabilities that cybercriminals can use? Are they willing to invest in research for making a robust system that can deal with these? While there is a rise in demand for personalized solutions, there's also heightened concern for privacy issues. How can organizations meet in the middle?

Whereas big techs need to work on technical solutions to fight this problem simultaneously, they also need to fight it from other angles. One of the essential steps is to appoint the right person who can create profound awareness among employees. The employees should know how getting into a trap of a faulty DF can affect their organization. If an organization wants to sustain in a future where DF attacks increase, they need to teach their teams how to detect such fake content. Organizations could also incorporate social engineering lessons for their people. There should be preparation done beforehand. Vulnerable areas that could be affected by DF should use detection algorithms. Risk handling is another concept that should be paid attention to while creating awareness. No matter how robust their algorithms are or how much people are aware, there are still chances that we can make mistakes [14]. Therefore, organizations' teams should know the following steps to undo the damage created. In addition to this, teams should know how to investigate the post-event impact of the mishap. There should be a well-guided team who can analyze the loss properly and see how much impact it has on the clients. Since this faulty activity is not a headache of just one company, all organizations should join hands and create a system to strengthen barriers that keep any synthesized content away. This system could be as a standard and then followed by other companies [15]. An accountable and responsible behavior from the organization's side can be a DF—safe environment.

## 11.7   FUTURE STRATEGIES: THROUGH SOCIETAL ASPECTS

Sure, a DF can be created against someone—an organization, person, community, etc. It might be their first responsibility to maintain a secure system that can't get hurt, but that doesn't mean that the users/consumers/society does not need being responsible. It might not be causing any direct harm to the individual watching it but his opinions or changed perspectives based on a piece of fake news. For example, a fake video of a politician won't harm the voter who watched it, but this voter's opinions influenced by that video can make him vote for the wrong person who is eventually bad for our society. In the future, incidents like this won't matter if our community is well guided and educated on such matters [16]. Media literacy is an essential factor in the spread and impact of a DF. Creating a media literate society will help people spot the difference between correct information and synthesized content. This model helps battle DF and the bizarre surprises that future technologies hold for us.

## 11.8   FUTURE STRATEGIES: THROUGH GOVERNMENTAL
##         ASPECTS

Governmental policies and involvement are just as significant. Governments should partner with organizations to invent effective technical solutions to combat this issue. One more aspect is spreading knowledge. Governments should be more clear and transparent to the public about whenever they are making use of DF in any of their campaigns or advertisements. It will be helpful in many ways. First, this will spread word about DFs to the audience of all age groups (even citizens) because most of all age groups watch the news (at least the news related to the government). Even if many people don't know what it means, at least this will make them curious about knowing what DF is. Second, this will introduce them to applications of DF and get familiar with how it is being popularized. Third, this will make them question any kind of media, stay aware, be responsible, and investigate before sharing any content further [17]. Furthermore, this will be a step forward in the media literacy of our society. It might also help encourage our community to dive into deep research and find solutions because as time passes, the quality of DFs will only get better.

## 11.9   SOCIAL MEDIA: A FUEL TO FORGED CONTENT?

Social media is the primary source of all of the content these days. Today, the content we consume primarily comes from the social media platforms. In India, every time riots happen, a lot of violence is fueled by forwarded WhatsApp messages and exaggerated videos delivered in excessive numbers. Once the public finds something bizarre or controversial, they share it with their knowns, and this cycle of forwarding content keeps going on. Most of the time, people don't even verify the authenticity of the content. Sometimes it is too real to doubt its authenticity. If the root cause is handled, it can stop so much damage from happening. This is where social media platforms and its actions come into play. Creating a detection system on social media platforms is not as easy as it may seem. It requires more robust algorithms which are designed very specifically. Why is it not easy? Because it is a tedious task to identify when to remove a DF and when to let it stay [18]. The problem is that social media platforms treat all kinds of problematic content the same. We know that not all DFs are faulty and controversial. Hence, they don't need to be taken down. Another problem is that not all untrue DFs are faulty.

Take this example: A person is not a good singer but using DFs; he has made himself sound good in a video. This isn't problematic and doesn't need to be taken down. Situations like this require the detection system to be precise. Also, it would be strange to target DFs while other fake content is available. Instances like these suggest that there is a need for a detection system that is precisely defined and has clear instructions. Identifying only "faulty," "problematic," or "malicious" DFs is a task and a challenge that needs to be taken care of in the future by social media platforms. If important policies are not regulated on time, it can result in the reduction of trust in news passed through Twitter, Facebook, or any other social media platform [19].

## 11.10   COMBATING WITH A "PRE-READY RESPONSE"

We cannot wait for a sudden miracle to happen, creating a 100% accurate detection system. It is a hot topic, and a lot of research is happening to figure out the ways to deal with it. When we don't have a detection system to rely on, it can be hard to verify or prove something wrong. This is why as a way to stay prepared for future attacks, an organization should focus on creating a response ahead of time. For example, if the synthesized content is circulated during an emergency, there won't be time to sit around and wait for it to go away because nothing can be done now. Understand it with this example: During riots, a flood, or even a cyclone, a video is circulated in which some reliable source is shown saying that everything is fine outside and nothing terrible is happening outdoors. Hearing this, people staying indoors might come out and get into trouble [20]. Now, there's no time to form a plan to undo things in a situation like this. It is the reason why organizations or anyone else should have an already set "plan of response." In this pre-ready response, they can have already set video scripts that can be circulated to explain to people what DF is, how it goes around, suggest some authentic sources, and state that they have not made it. It will help expose the controversy and prevent further damage. It is essential because the longer it stays in news without a response, the longer it will be in the circulation loop. The sooner a clarity response is given, the better. Maintaining data of event recordings that involve being on camera or public speaking can be used as proof when such a situation arises. It can verify your response statement and undo the damage to much extent.

Whereas it is essential to respond as soon as possible, it is also necessary to identify this malicious act in time [21]. The sooner we get to know that there is a DF, the better for us. It is hard to spot it because the people who are creating it try to keep it away from the sights of the concerned person. In a future full of DFs, the organizations can use emergency or alert bots. How will it work? It will focus on people in the organization who stay on cameras and send an alert every time they find something concerning this person. It can be news articles, random blogs, or social media platforms. If you identify that people are talking about this person through hashtags or in comments, it indicates something is wrong.

## 11.11 LEGAL SYSTEM AND POLICIES (ACROSS DIFFERENT NATIONS)

Earlier, we read about the regulations passed by the European Union regarding data rights. The governments of all countries must start intervening by creating new rules and policies. It will build a legal framework that will give the society some direction, including the inventors of such content. Let's learn what the other governments are doing to fight against this.

Few countries have created regulations against content that spreads misinformation. USA, UK, Australia, and China are a few of them. But do these laws alone have the capability of handling the high-level fakeablity of DF content? In 2019, the USA laid out law for combating DFs. According to this law, it is mandatory to add a watermark to synthesized content to be identified easily. In addition to this, Virginia passed a law that implements criminal charges over a person who distributes pornographic DF videos without the consent of the person in it. Texas is another example of a law that restricts/bans the creation of any DF content that is faulty and problematic to political issues.

In 2019, California banned the use of DF content related to politicians before 60 days of elections to prevent any misleading content. Whereas there's no natural law against DF in India, a law (passed in 2019) ensures the data protection rights of a person and restricts the usage of an individual's data. It gives protection to some extent, but there's no law protecting the data of a person who is not alive anymore. It is a very well-known fact that India has a very vast political system—lots of parties pitched against each other, everyday battles, showing others in a bad light are just a few aspects. In such an environment, DF can create a blunder. For instance, a manipulated video of a dead person from party A can create a big controversy and shake the public's beliefs [22]. It will make party A look terrible in the public eyes. It is why specific laws for a dead person's data protection should also exist. For similar scenarios, a Spanish law was also passed in 2018, giving the "right to erase content" to the heir of the dead person. Yes, these laws do not directly focus on DF content, but it gives some safety. The future will tell how effective these laws will be because the internet is a vast space which makes it hard to predict anything. With all these laws of different countries, China went one step ahead. In its earlier policies in 2019, China banned the distribution of misinformation and false content, which was created using AI techniques, including VR. The new rules go one step ahead and impose a ban over any app which pushes forged or compromised content toward its users using high-quality algorithms. It ensures that the social media platforms which use robust algorithms to provide customized content don't spread fake content to the users. These extend mainly toward the news platforms. Any social media app cannot allow manipulated content under this law in China. This law also puts pressure on the creators of other social media platforms. Collaborative steps to form regulations can also be helpful [23]. It'll make sense in some cases where information is being passed across multiple borders (since some of the platforms exist globally). It may become more complex to detect and understand in the future. Passing laws is essential and can prove effective because this technology is still in its initial phase.

## 11.12    IS DEEPFAKES HERE TO STAY OR NOT?/FUTURE FORECAST

Well, there is no direct and sure answer to this question. By looking at all the issues and positive applications connected to it, we can interpret that this technology can take three paths—positive, negative, or even-handed. Only the future will unravel whether or not having only positive impacts is possible. It seems pretty hard (not completely impossible) on today's date. Having this scenario in the future might be possible with strict frameworks and regulations. If DFs are used positively, they can create limitless opportunities and applications. A few of the areas are the entertainment industry (including movies), next-level personalization (enhancing customer relationship), celebrity advertisements, fashion industry, social media, dubbing (for movies or ads), gaming industry, educational purposes, or even the healthcare sector. It will be a best-case scenario [24]. The worst-case scenario is possible if all the measures are not taken properly. It can happen when security is not tight. It can lead to a future full of scams, impersonation of public figures (celebrities and politicians), loss of money, creating trust issues, violation of personal data, fake IDs, etc. It will lead to distrusting AI as a whole system [25]. The third case that is very likely to happen somewhat lies in both negative and positive. It is the current state of it—negatives and positives simultaneously [26].

## 11.13    FUTURE EXPECTATIONS FROM DEEPFAKE

Like other AI techniques have made their way in our everyday lives, we can expect the same with DFs. It is understandable if someone says that AI will play a huge part in the entertainment and media industry in the future. Even though it has already started paving its way into the marketing sector through commercials and other marketing techniques, we can expect much more in the upcoming years. Keeping its dark side aside, we are aware that it is a game-changing tool to bring consumers closer to the seller and its brand because it creates a win-win situation for both. AI is accepted by the society because of its ease in daily tasks.

Similarly, DFs will help the seller by easing up the task of creating personalized and customized marketing for its variety of customers. Many researchers are involved in inventing new areas to make use of this technology. One of the areas is the gaming industry. It is expected to make the most use out of this technology. People creating games have struggled to make them look close to reality for a long time. Every gamer's fantasy has super-realistic visuals in a game.

DFs makes it seem possible. Having a celebrity's face on their player, realistic body movements, real-time expressions, or even realistic objects in the background will make the experience great for any gamer. It will help in reducing costs for production. Not just the existing gamer community, but it will also attract new users. Another surprising sector under research is healthcare. The idea is to create a patient and his health data using DF. It can be used for testing for various treatment purposes. Using it can be good as actual patients won't have to go through any testing and its side effects. On top of this, there will be no use of accurate data, which is the primary concern with DFs.

Once the wrong side of this technology starts getting negated, people will start accepting it. It has immense potential of being used in creative and unique applications. Let's wait to see how things roll in the coming years!

## REFERENCES

[1]  Somers, M., DFs, explained https://mitsloan.mit.edu/ideas-made-to-matter/DFs-explai ned (Accessed on August 17, 2021).

[2]  Cole, S. (24 January 2018). "We Are Truly Fucked: Everyone Is Making AI-Generated Fake Porn Now." Vice. Archived from the original on 7 September 2019. Retrieved 4 May 2019.

[3]  Karnouskos, S. (Sept. 2020). "AIin Digital Media: The Era of DFs," in *IEEE Transactions on Technology and Society*, Vol. 1, No. 3, pp. 138–147. doi:10.1109/TTS.2020.3001312

[4]  Thies, J., Zollhöfer, M., Stamminger, M., Theobalt, C., and Nießner, M. Face2Face: Realtime Face Capture and Reenactment of RGB Videos" and was published in Proc. Computer Vision and Pattern Recognition (CVPR), 2016, IEEE. doi:10.1145/3292039

[5]  Thies, J., Zollhöfer, M., Stamminger, M., Theobalt, C., and Nießner, M. (January 2019). Open Collaboration in an Age of Distrust, Communications of the ACM, Vol. 62, No. 1, pp. 96–104. doi:10.1145/3292039

[6]  Vaccari, C., and Chadwick, A. DFs and Disinformation: Exploring the Impact of Synthetic Political Video on Deception, Uncertainty, and Trust in News, Volume: 6, Issue: 1, https://doi.org/10.1177/2056305120903408

[7]  www.tcs.com/content/dam/tcs/pdf/discover-tcs/Research-and-Innovation/Deepfakes-Envisioning-Prospects-and-Perils.pdf) (Accessed on August 17, 2021).

[8]  https://restofworld.org/2022/china-steps-up-efforts-to-ban-deepfakes/ (Accessed on August 17, 2021).

[9] https://interculturaltalk.com/2019/11/05/cool-but-scaryDFs-are-here/ (Accessed on August 17, 2021).

[10] https://medium.com/@songda/a-short-history-of-DFs-604ac7be6016 (Accessed on August 17, 2021).

[11] www.discovermagazine.com/technology/DFs-the-dark-origins-of-fake-videos-and-their-potential-to-wreak-havoc (Accessed on August, 17, 2021).

[12] https://medium.com/predict/why-deepfakes-will-make-you-play-video-games-instead-of-movies-99ee5c2d7c9e (Accessed on August 17, 2021).

[13] www.technologyreview.com/2020/12/24/1015380/best-ai-DFs-of-2020/ (Accessed on August 17, 2021).

[14] www.thinkautomation.com/bots-and-ai/ai-in-healthcare-how-artificial-intelligence-can-help-us-fight- (Accessed on August 20, 2021).

[15] Sharma, D. K., Gaur, L., and Okunbor, D. (2007). "Image compression and feature extraction with neural network," Proceedings of the Academy of Information and Management Sciences, Vol. 11, No. 1, pp. 33–38.

[16] Anshu, K., Gaur, L., and Khazanchi, D. (2017). "Evaluating satisfaction level of grocery E-retailers using intuitionistic fuzzy TOPSIS and ECCSI model," *International Conference on Infocom Technologies and Unmanned Systems (Trends and Future Directions) (ICTUS)*, pp. 276–284, doi:10.1109/ICTUS.2017.8286019

[17] Gaur, L., and Anshu, K. (2018). Consumer preference analysis for websites using e-TailQ and AHP. International Journal of Engineering & Technology, Vol. 7, No. 2.11, pp. 14–20.

[18] Rana, J., Gaur, L., Singh, G., Awan, U., and Rasheed, M.I. (2021). Reinforcing customer journey through artificial intelligence: A review and research agenda. International Journal of Emerging Markets, Vol. ahead-of-print (No. ahead-of-print). https://doi.org/10.1108/IJOEM-08-2021-1214

[19] Gaur, L., Singh, G., Solanki, A., Jhanjhi, N. Z., Bhatia, U., Sharma, S., ... and Kim, W. (2021), Disposition of youth in predicting sustainable development goals using the neuro-fuzzy and random forest algorithms. Human-Centric Computing and Information Sciences, 11, NA.

[20] Singh, G., Kumar, B., Gaur, L., and Tyagi, A. (2019). "Comparison between Multinomial and Bernoulli Naïve Bayes for Text Classification," *2019 International Conference on Automation, Computational and Technology Management (ICACTM)*, pp. 593–596. doi:10.1109/ICACTM.2019.8776800

[21] Gaur, L., Agarwal, V., and Anshu, K. (2020). "Fuzzy DEMATEL Approach to Identify the Factors Influencing Efficiency of Indian Retail," Strategic System Assurance and Business Analytics. Asset Analytics (Performance and Safety Management). Springer, Singapore. https://doi.org/10.1007/978-981-15-3647-2_

[22] Gaur, L., Afaq, A., Singh, G., and Dwivedi, YK (2021). Role of artificial intelligence and robotics to foster the touchless travel during a pandemic: A review and research agenda. International Journal of Contemporary Hospitality Management, Vol. 33, No. 11, pp. 4079–4098. https://doi.org/10.1108/IJCHM-11-2020-1246

[23] Sharma, S., Singh, G., Gaur, L., and Sharma, R. (2022). Does psychological distance and religiosity influence fraudulent customer behaviour? International Journal of Consumer Studies. doi:10.1111/ijcs.12773

[24] Sahu, G., Gaur, L., and Singh, G. (2021). Applying niche and gratification theory approach to examine the users' indulgence towards over-the-top platforms and conventional TV. Telematics and Informatics, 65. doi:10.1016/j.tele.2021.101713

[25] Ramakrishnan, R., Gaur, L., and Singh, G. (2016). Feasibility and efficacy of BLE beacon IoT devices in inventory management at the shop floor. International Journal of Electrical and Computer Engineering, 6(5), 2362–2368. doi:10.11591/ijece. v6i5.10807

[26] Afaq, A., Gaur, L., Singh, G., and Dhir, A. (2021). COVID-19: Transforming air passengers' behaviour and reshaping their expectations towards the airline industry. Tourism Recreation Research. doi:10.1080/02508281.2021.2008211

# Index

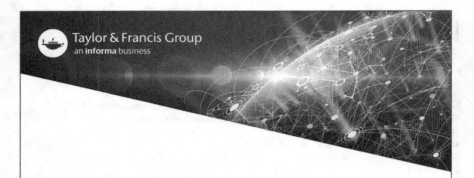

Printed in the United States
by Baker & Taylor Publisher Services